L.Campau's House
Junius D.Hatch's Addition 80
The City of Grand Rapids is 40 miles above the mouth of the Grand River; which is navigable for Steam Boats drawing 3 feet water to said Village and Boats of the ordinary size used on canals now ascend to the mouth of the Maple River a distance of 60 miles above the Rapids.
By J.Almy. Civil Engineer Scale 400 Feet to an Inch.
RANSOM
BOSTWICK St 66 Ft
DIVISION St 66 Ft
Court House Square
LAGRAVE
SHELDON St 66 Ft
SPRING St 66 Ft
PRAIRIE
ALMY St 66 Ft
CALDER St 66 Ft
SUMMIT St 100 Ft
WATER St 66 Ft
BRIDGE St
BRONSON St
LYON St
PEARL St
FOUNTAIN St
GREEN
JUSTICE
MONROE St
WATER
LOUIS
FERRY
OFFICIAL St
FULTON St
ISLAND St
OAKES St
ELLSWORTH St
Basin 200 ft Square
Lock St
GRAND RIVER
Ferry
Mission 46 17/100
Sibleys
Mission
Bridge Street Road
Section line
Road to Thornapple
Road

Pictorial History of
GRAND RAPIDS

Pictorial History of
GRAND RAPIDS

by Lynn G. Mapes
and Anthony Travis

with illustrations by
Reynold Weidenaar

KREGEL PUBLICATIONS
Grand Rapids, Michigan 49501

International Standard Book Number 0-8254-3213-8

Library of Congress Catalog Card Number 75-8015

First Edition, 1976

Printed in the United States of America

Dedicated to
Dolly, Martha, and Dorothy.
—L. G. M.

For Professor Madison Kuhn
from whom I have learned much
and for Marc Travis
from whom I will learn much.
—A. T.

CONTENTS

THE WHITE HOUSE

WASHINGTON

February 23, 1976

Dear Friends:

Betty and I are happy to have this opportunity to include our own message of congratulations in this Pictorial History commemorating Grand Rapids' Bicentennial-Sesquicentennial celebration.

We cherish our ties with Grand Rapids, and at this important time in its history, we feel a special closeness. There will be much said in the days ahead about our city's rich heritage, its proud past. There will be a lot said, too, about the future for ours is a city of creative and industrious people. This book contains these facts. However, as longtime residents of Grand Rapids, there is another fact we are especially happy to share. It is a fact reflected in these pages. More importantly it is reflected in the homes, the businesses, the churches, the schools; it is reflected on the faces of the people, it is demonstrated thousands of ways every day. Quite simply, it is the spirit of concern and caring the citizens of Grand Rapids have for each other as well as for their city.

Our hearts are with you during this year of celebration.

Sincerely,

Gerald R. Ford

Authors' Preface

This book is primarily a social history of a people and their urban environment. It is a pioneering effort in that it is a photographic collection organized to illustrate and enlarge upon the major themes of city development. These include the growth of a concentrated central business district and its decline, the extension of a municipal transportation system, the maturation of an economic base, the transfer of various urban services from the private to the public sector, the rise of heterogeneous neighborhoods, and the expansion of local recreational opportunities. One of the few books in this area is the fine study by H. M. Mayer and Richard Wade, *Chicago: The Growth of a Metropolis.* It proved to be of great value. We have, however, tried to put more emphasis on people and less on urban structures.

The value of such a method is that it allows the viewer to explore the history of Grand Rapids, a middle-sized city in the midwest, with his or her visual sense. New perceptions are formed that are not as readily available through the written word. It is for this reason that the text has been kept to a minimum. The major themes of urban life should be apparent from the pictures themselves. Only essential identifications have been made along with rough guidelines to some possible interpretations.

As the reader will understand, many of the older photographs are not of the best quality. Films and photographic papers used in the past, plus years of handling, have taken their toll. However, the old photographs were often too interesting not to include, despite their imperfect condition.

One of the limitations of a visual approach to social history is the lack of a wide range of photographs. In this case the opposite was true. The main task was to reduce to a usable number the almost countless pictures in the two major collections at the Grand Rapids Public Library and the Grand Rapids Public Museum. Thomas Genson and Francis Collins at the library and Gordon Olson at the museum provided invaluable advice and aid. The Grand Rapids Historical Commission, which brought together professional historians and the community, cannot be thanked too much. The authors also wish to thank Catherine Cuti for her ambitious and perceptive work on layout and copy editing. In addition, Bonnie Jean Travis did the initial copy editing and typing of the manuscript. Most of the pictures in the last chapter were taken by Craig Vander Lende.

Bridge-Looking Northeast

Downtown

In 1826 the fur trader, Louis Campau, built a trading post on the site of the square that bears his name today. Around Grab Corners, as the early settlers called Campau Square, Grand Rapids grew into a thriving city. For almost a century, downtown Grand Rapids was the city's center of almost all finance, commerce, and entertainment. These have now been diffused throughout a much larger metropolitan area as suburbs have expanded and easily accessible shopping malls have prospered. But downtown Grand Rapids is still the heart of the city.

Rev. John Booth's sketch of the site that was to become Grand Rapids, 1831. In the foreground is Chief Noonday's camp. On the same side of the river at right is Campau's cabin and trading post; on the opposite shore is the Baptist mission.

In November of 1826 Louis Campau, the "father of Grand Rapids", built a temporary shelter among the Indians camped at the future site of the city. The following year the fur trapper and trader, apparently having decided to settle down, constructed a log cabin and trading post and soon brought his wife, Sophia, from Detroit.

Louis Campau.

Indian trails led to and from this spot on the banks near the rapids in the river the Indians called Owashtanong, "the faraway waters". On the west shore opposite Campau's post was Rev. Isaac McCoy's Baptist mission, established in 1823 to try to "civilize" and to convert to Christianity the Ottawa Indians who used the area as a meeting and resting place. Eighteenth century conflicts between the Indians and the whites had already considerably reduced the number of Indians in the area; with the further encroachment of new settlers the remaining Indians were quietly moved westward. Almost all the Indians were gone by 1837 and the Baptist mission was closed.

Meanwhile, Louis Campau had purchased seventy-two acres of land for ninety dollars in 1831; this land would become the central business district of Grand Rapids. His property was bounded by the present streets of Michigan on the north, Fulton on the south, Division on the east, and the Grand River on the west. Campau added a blacksmith shop to his trading post and the village of Grand Rapids was born.

No. 723 RECEIVER'S OFFICE, WESTERN DISTRICT, M. T.

White Pigeon, 20th Sept. 1831

RECEIVED from Louis Campau Jun. of Kalamazoo Co. M. Ty the sum of Ninety Dollars and — Cents, being in full for the North East fraction of Section No. 25 in Township No. 7 North of range No. Twelve West, containing Seventy two acres, at the rate of $1,25 per acre. $ 90.00

Receiver.

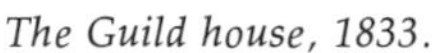

The Guild house, 1833.

Joel Guild.

After a government survey in 1833, Campau sold Joel Guild the first two lots on what was to become Monroe Avenue. On this land which cost him forty-five dollars, Guild built the first frame house in this area and thus began the permanent settlement of Grand Rapids. Today the McKay Tower stands on the old Guild House site.

The photograph below of Waterloo Street (Market Avenue today), from one of the earliest existing glass plate negatives of downtown Grand Rapids, was taken in 1857. A census taken in 1850, the year the village drew up its first city charter, showed a population of of 2,686. The town was still small — photographed from the corner at Monroe, open fields and woods are visible at the end of the street, only a block long. But signs of growth and progress are also evident in the carefully leveled road, wooden sidewalks, good-sized frame buildings, and two hotels — the Eagle Hotel at right, where the Kalamazoo stagecoach line stopped three times per week, and Barnard House further down the street.

Waterloo Street, 1857.

The old Guild house in this reproduction of an 1852 daguerreotype has been partially turned around and has become a meat market. This is one of the earliest pictorial representations of Grab Corners, which was later to be called Campau Square, the focal point of the downtown business district.

Campau Square was formed quite by accident. Two rival property holders, Lucius Lyon who after 1836 owned the land north of Pearl Street and Louis Campau who owned the acreage to the south, could not agree on a common street plan. One result was that Monroe Avenue did not cross Pearl Street in the early days.

Grab Corners, 1873.

Even when the street was cut through the blocking buildings, thus joining Monroe Avenue to Canal Street (now Lower Monroe), there was a jog in the street which necessitated two forty-five degree turns. In 1873 the buildings on Monroe off Pearl, in the photograph at left below, were torn down, creating the "square". The picture at right below shows Campau Square in 1874 after the renovation. On the left is the Sweet Hotel which later became the Pantlind.

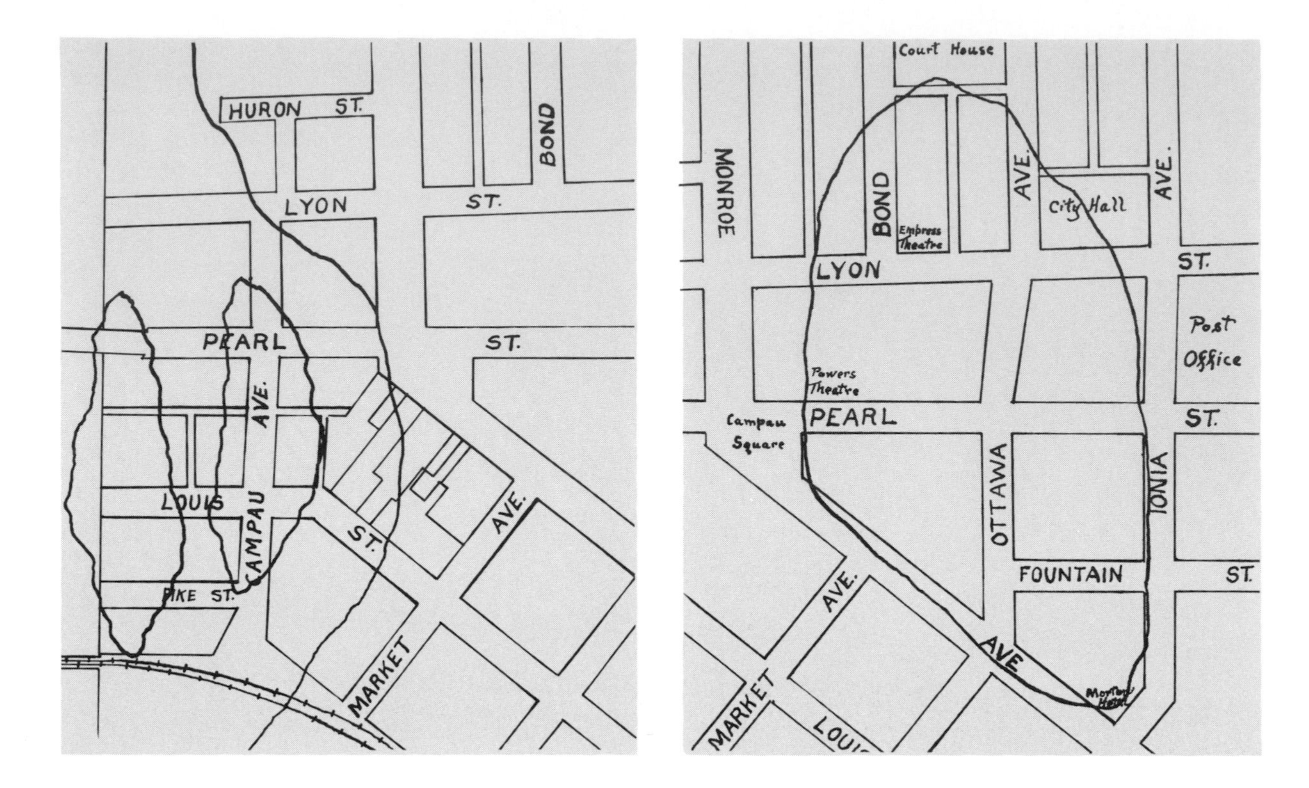

The early settlers literally rebuilt the terrain to form the downtown area. The map at left above shows that the river originally extended right into what is now Campau Square; much of the land now occupied by the Pantlind Hotel and surrounding buildings was at first under the waters of the Grand. As nearby hills were leveled the soil was used to fill in the river channels between and around the islands and the shore, finally shaping the riverbank as it exists today.

All along the shore of the Grand the land was hilly. Streets such as Market (Waterloo) Avenue were raised several feet to the level of Monroe. Louis Campau laid out Monroe Avenue along an old Indian trail that hugged the southwest base of Prospect Hill, which rose forty feet above the present street level. The irregular shape in the center of the map at right above shows the extent of Prospect Hill. A comparison of these maps with the primeval terrain map on page 88 gives a good idea of how Grand Rapids appeared to the early settlers and the enormous effort they put into building the city.

George B. Morton, an early resident of Grand Rapids, built this house on Prospect Hill at the northwest corner of Ottawa and Pearl, in the block that is now the site of the Waters Building. As were many such residences built close to the heart of town, it was torn down as the central business district expanded. Prospect Hill itself was eventually leveled, the soil from the hill providing much of the fill dirt needed at the river and in the crooked streets.

The early business district radiated outward from Campau Square. The picture at left, taken around 1875, shows Pearl Street west of Monroe with the covered bridge over the Grand in the background. Below is an 1875 view up Monroe from Campau Square. A single track for a horse-drawn streetcar was the beginning of public transportation in Grand Rapids.

A shopper downtown in this era could select from a wide variety of dry goods, produce, and groceries, visit a doctor, dentist or lawyer, take care of his or her banking needs, and also enjoy a restaurant meal, perhaps at the Cosmopolitan (below) just north of Campau Square on Canal Street.

By the 1870's Campau Square and Monroe Avenue were the heart of a thriving business district. Not only was the population clustered close-by, but all the streetcars were routed downtown. It was, therefore, convenient to shop on Monroe with no "parking problems". On the left in this 1880's photograph of Sweet's Hotel in Campau Square is the famous Monroe Avenue clock, which was destroyed when Woolworth's built a new store on the site in 1939.

At right is a late 1800's view from Peck's Drugstore on the corner of Monroe and North Division. The picture below looking up Monroe from Campau Square was taken in 1897. On the left is the Wonderly Building. The photograph demonstrates the vitality of the downtown area with the sidewalks filled with people and the streets crowded with trolley cars.

These four pictures of the southeast corner of Monroe and Pearl demonstrate the growth of the city. The first photograph dates from the late 1860's. By the time the second photograph was taken in the 1890's the Wonderly Building, built in 1888, had replaced several of the earlier structures on the corner. In 1915-16 the first two stories of the Grand Rapids National Bank building were erected on the site and in 1926-27 fourteen more stories were added (third and fourth photographs). The bank did not survive the financial crash of the 1930's. Frank D. McKay, a prominent Grand Rapids businessman and politician, purchased the structure and rechristened it McKay Tower, an office building which still stands on the site today.

Campau Square decorated for the Centennial, 1876.

Sending off the troops to the Spanish-American War, April, 1898.

Campau Square, in the heart of the city, has served as a gathering place and focal point for many events and celebrations through the years.

Soapbox oratory, Campau Square, 1920's.

Before the advent of the automobile and suburban living, the central business district of a city the size of Grand Rapids was the hub of many activities. These included government, entertainment, commerce, banking, and professional services. Essential to a thriving downtown was a healthy hotel business. By 1890 there were more than forty hotels that could accommodate over three thousand people. In those days before mass communication and speedy transportation, it was often necessary for commercial and other visitors to stay in Grand Rapids more than one day to complete their business.

By no means the first hotel, but certainly the most enduring, was the Sweet (Pantlind) Hotel. In 1868 Martin L. Sweet built his hotel on the northwest corner of Monroe and Pearl. It was purchased by J. Boyd Pantlind in 1902, who quickly turned it into the leading hotel in town. A "new", completely rebuilt, Pantlind was finished in 1924. With 750 rooms it became the host of many conventions, including a 1920's Grand Army of the Republic gathering. With the completion of the Civic Auditorium across the street, the Pantlind has continued to thrive as a regional convention center. The photographs on this page, from top to bottom, were taken in 1910, mid-1920's and 1930.

The Eagle Hotel, Grand Rapids' first, was built in 1834 on the northwest corner of Waterloo (Market) and Louis. This hotel was especially popular with temperance visitors, for it contained no bar.

The frame building burned to the ground in 1883 and was rebuilt in brick. The new structure contained ninety rooms furnished by the local manufacturer, Berkey & Gay.
The inn failed to survive the Great Depression and closed its doors in 1934.

In 1834 Louis Campau built a home on the southwest corner of Waterloo (Market) and Monroe. In 1838, after finishing an addition to the building, he rented it to two sisters who operated a boarding house. Charles Rathbun made further improvements in 1846 and opened the Rathbun House. Like other large hotels in early Grand Rapids, it was one of the cultural and entertainment centers for the city.

The Rathbun House contained a large dining room and a ballroom on the upper floor used for concerts, lectures, and traveling theater. The Rathbun and other hotels also served as meeting halls for political and civic organizations, and reception centers for weddings and other celebrations and commemorations.

The National Hotel, 1870.

Another important hotel tradition was begun in 1835 when Hiram Hindsill erected the Hindsill Hotel at Monroe and Ionia. It later became the National Hotel and then the Morton House. Immediately after an 1873 fire it was rebuilt of brick. This was a familiar pattern for many downtown structures. In fact, fire became almost a common, if unintentional, tool of urban renewal.

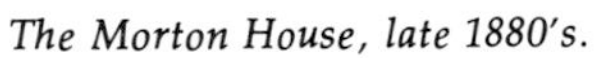

The Morton House, late 1880's.

Commerce was the lifeblood of downtown Grand Rapids. Antoine Campau, a brother of Louis, opened the first "general store" in 1837 in Grab Corners. He sold everything from groceries to wines to dry goods. By the 1860's the days of the general store were numbered as the retail trade began to specialize. Dry goods "department" stores began to sprout up downtown. In 1862, for example, J. H. Doornink and Paul Steketee formed a partnership to operate the mercantile establishment at the far right in this photograph. In 1872 Doornink retired and sold his share of the business to Steketee. In 1878, Steketee's moved from Canal Street to its present location on Upper Monroe, the "main street" of Grand Rapids.

Steketee's, although it has expanded to Eastbrook Mall, has maintained its store downtown. Wurzburg's, on the other hand, opened several branches in the suburban malls and closed its downtown store. Frederick W. Wurzburg opened his first store, at the right in this photograph, in 1872 on Canal Street. The store remained on Lower Monroe for seventy-nine years until 1951 when it moved into a building at the corner of Monroe and Ottawa, recently vacated by Herpolsheimer's. With the increasing success of the suburban malls, Wurzburg's abandoned its downtown location in the early 1970's.

Herpolsheimer's remains downtown although, like Steketee's, it has opened a suburban branch. This 1920 photograph shows Herp's at its original location on Monroe and Ottawa, later occupied by Wurzburg's. Herpolsheimer's opened here in 1881, moved several times to different spots on Monroe and finally settled in 1949 in its modernized building in the wedge formed by Fulton, Division and Monroe.

Several stores with long histories in downtown Grand Rapids, still located there today, can be seen in this 1920's photograph. Houseman's, the oldest clothing store in Grand Rapids, is still at the site where it was opened in 1852. Others are Siegel Jewelry, Woolworth's, and Kresge's. Another historic clothing store, not in the photograph, is May's, located at Lower Monroe and Lyon since 1883.

Two important retail stores on Monroe that did not survive were Friedman-Spring's Dry Goods (later M. Friedman & Co.), established in 1854, and the Boston Store, established in 1885. Although both prospered at one time, the depression forced Friedman's out of business in 1930, while shifting retail sales patterns led the Boston Store into bankruptcy in 1951.

Grand opening of the F. W. Grand store, with the Boston Store at left and Friedman-Spring's at right.

Very early buildings downtown were often constructed in such a way as to make the space above ground level unusable. As business increased, however, the city built up as well as out and taller structures became the norm. The building in this photograph followed a familiar pattern with a jewelry store and a restaurant occupying the street level and several dentists, a chiropodist, a tailor, and a hairdresser upstairs.

Expanding suburbs around the city along with the development of the expressway systems seriously weakened the downtown area as a commercial center. As they moved to the suburbs, many people no longer wished to shop in the central business district. Store owners along with service and professional people accommodated them by locating in malls and shopping centers around the periphery of the city. Plans are currently underway to make the downtown area more accessible and attractive to today's shopper.

Downtown Grand Rapids, however, still has an historical feeling that cannot be recaptured in the contemporary malls and shopping centers. While most interiors and some exteriors have been remodeled, enough original architecture remains in the downtown area that it is still easy to imagine the time when one could shop or eat in the stores pictured here and on the following page.

Old Grand Rapids was a good place for a busy shopper to find a bite to eat or something to drink, whether one wanted a quick lunch in a cafeteria, a sweet with coffee or tea, or a Welch's grape juice.

Firehouse at Chester and Diamond

Government Serves the People

The early settlers of Grand Rapids, like the inhabitants of most frontier communities, were responsible for their own well-being. Each household provided its members with protection against crime, fire, and disease, insured an adequate supply of fresh water, disposed of its garbage, and so forth. As the community grew in size and complexity, the self-sufficient life style of the settlers necessarily gave way to public, collective action.

By the turn of the century, the city government was providing to the citizens many services, most of them essential to their safety, health, and well-being. The chart below, comparing the expenditures of the city in 1922 with those of 1902, outlines these services. Some had been the responsibility of the government from early village days. Others were first provided only through individual effort or private enterprise. Gradually, as the city continued to grow, and as efficient and equitable delivery of essential services through private sources became unwieldy, more of the basic needs of the people became public responsibility.

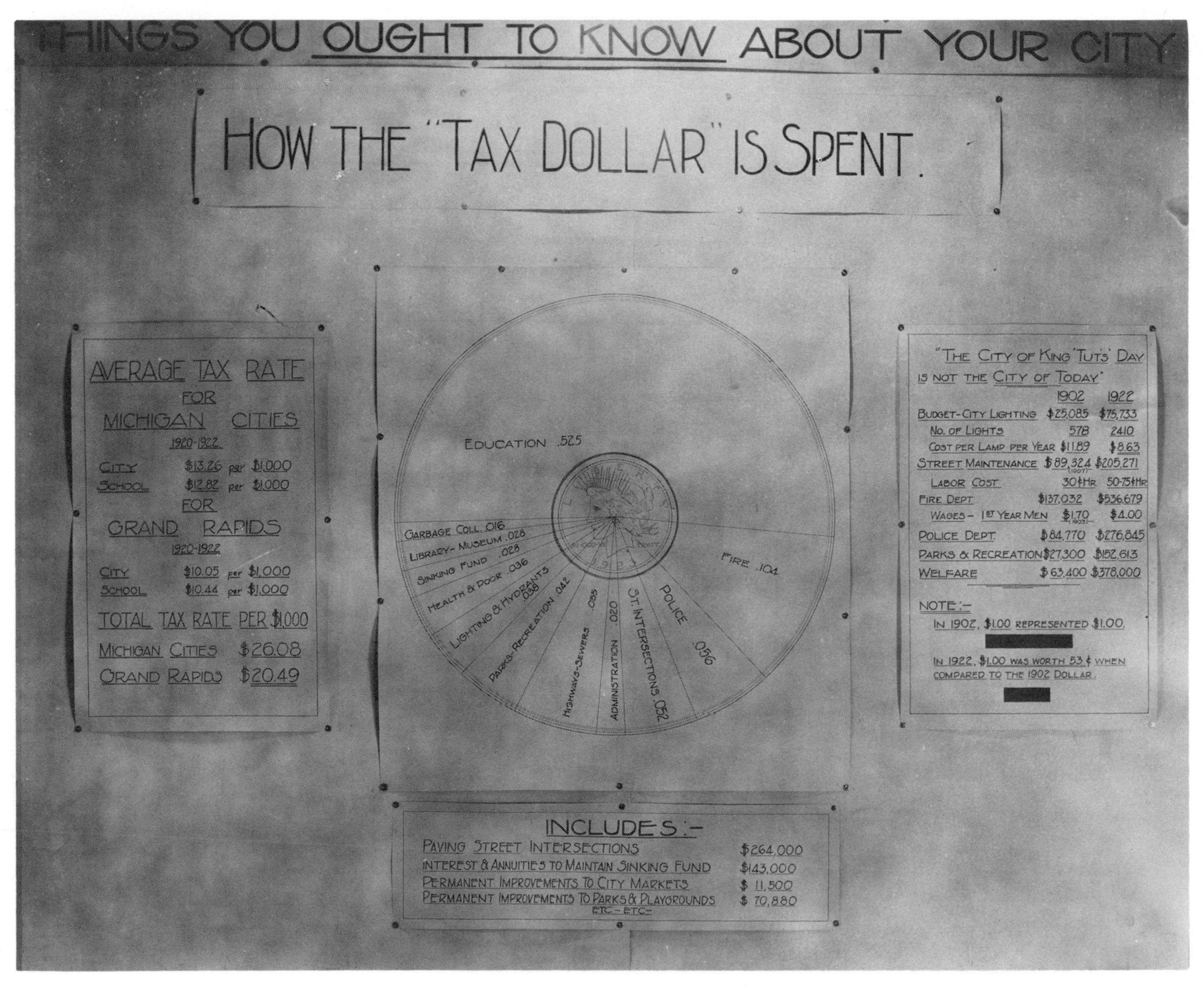

Police headquarters, about 1897.

A good example of this process was the development of police protection. In the earliest village days of Grand Rapids, the hardy male settler with his fowling piece assumed primary responsibility for the protection of his family and property. In addition, the mayor as the chief law enforcer, and the city councilmen with the power to arrest, were accountable for public order. To aid them, the citizens elected constables who served without pay, and earned their livelihood in other full-time occupations. By 1856, when Grand Rapids had achieved a population of 7,000 and the reputation of a rather rowdy lumberjack town, it became evident that to maintain order, especially at night, it would be necessary to hire a full-time professional peace officer. Despite this early beginning it was not until 1871 that the city created a professional police department.

In 1892, the city completed construction of a building at the corner of Ottawa and Crescent to house the police department. Although an addition was already necessary by 1914, and by the 1950's the department had overflowed into nearby buildings, it occupied this building until moving into the new Civic Center complex in 1966.

Grand Rapids patrolmen, 1907.

Before the widespread introduction of the impersonal squad car in the 1940's, most patrolling was done on foot on a regular beat. The uniformed police officer on his rounds met the people of the neighborhood on a daily basis, thus becoming an integral part of their lives.

"Black Maria" at the Ottawa Street entrance, police headquarters.

Patrol wagons, known by various nicknames such as "Black Maria" and "Free Ride Wagon", were used to transport policemen to the scene of a public disorder and to cart criminals, drunks, and other troublemakers off to jail.

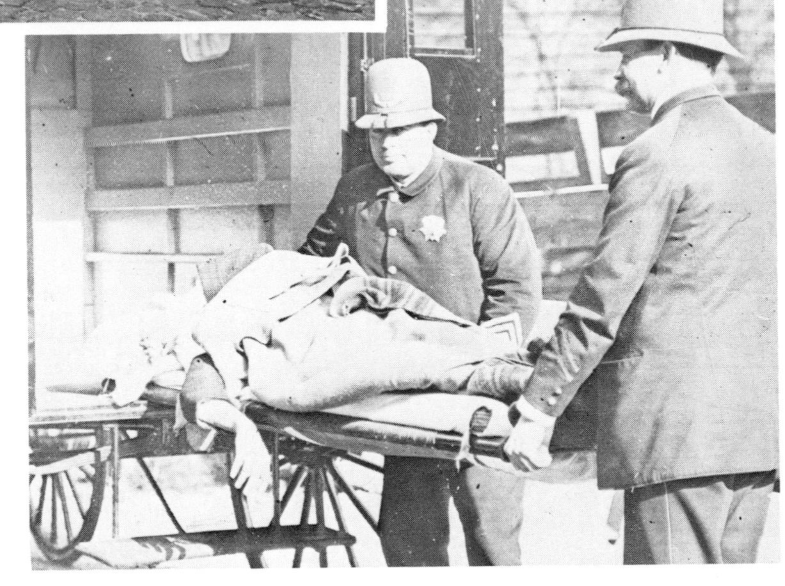

The police not only protected the community from crime, but also performed important safety duties. The policeman directing traffic for the schoolchildren no doubt also formed friendships with them.

Fire was a constant danger in early settlement days when most construction materials were highly inflammable. All inhabitants with their water buckets were expected to lend a hand in fighting any conflagrations. As the town grew, this haphazard and confused system of many individuals throwing water on a blaze proved to be increasingly inadequate. In the 1840's businessmen with property to protect took the lead in forming volunteer fire companies.

Wolverine Fire Company No. 3, Grab Corners (later Campau Square), 1860.

The advantage of volunteer fire companies was that they could purchase equipment and train their members to act in unison. The first equipment consisted of water buckets and small hand-drawn, hand-pumped "engines" which could produce a jet of water several stories high. A bucket brigade supplied the engine by pouring water into the tank while a group of men pumped it out by hand. The pumping was backbreaking work requiring two crews, one to relieve the other. In the mid-1860's firefighting took a step forward with the introduction of steam engines to pump water. The earliest models did not throw water any further than the older machines, but at least relieved the men of the exhausting labor of hand pumping.

As the stores and hotels in the central business district became taller and larger and the factories along the Grand River expanded, the city began to plan for a professional fire department financed by the public. It would consist of men who were highly trained, were on call at all times, and had access to the latest firefighting equipment. This goal was not fully accomplished until the turn of the century. In 1900 the city fire department consisted of 124 men, 23 pieces of equipment, and 54 horses.

In the 1860's Grand Rapids firefighters had begun to use horses to pull the fire wagons. For half a century these herculean fire horses, racing at breakneck speed, ably accomplished their assigned task of fetching the firemen and their equipment to the scene of a blaze.

Hose cart on Bridge St. during the flood of March, 1904.

Progress finally made the noble steed obsolete despite his loyal service. In 1910 a hose cart was equipped with an internal combustion engine and from then on the city motorized the fire department as the budget permitted. In 1921 the last of the fire horses were transferred to the garbage-hauling detail, to the great disgust of many of the firemen who had admired and cared for them.

Disappointment at the disappearance of the fire horse must soon have been replaced by respect for the advantages of the motorized fire trucks with their capability of transporting heavier, improved equipment at previously unheard of speed.

Grading Ottawa Avenue, from Pearl to Monroe, 1865.

Streets and roads were a matter of public concern from earliest village days. Two of the city's "founding fathers", Louis Campau and Lucius Lyon, were responsible for the original laying out of the streets in what became the central business district. As early as 1841 the village government authorized a tax levy of $172.38 for improvements on Division and Monroe avenues, and ever since the city has been primarily responsible for the maintenance of the roadways. Development of the city streets, including the removal of the stumps of felled trees, grading and filling, and solving drainage problems, was a time-consuming and backbreaking process.

Snowplow, early 1920's model.

1917-model street sweeper.

Upkeep was also an enormous task. Prior to the invention of motorized and mechanized equipment, such as the snowplow and street sweeper in these photographs, men wielding shovels and brooms worked to keep the streets usable and clean.

The old city waterworks at Monroe and Coldbrook.

Early settlers in the area found an abundant supply of clear, fresh water. Growth of the town, along with the inevitable contamination of water supplies, soon made it difficult for individuals to obtain enough clean water to meet their needs. From 1848 to 1873, the privately owned Grand Rapids Hydraulic Company supplied most of the water to the city residents. By 1873 the company's service was inadequate and the city decided to set up its own water system. Both the Hydraulic Company, which obtained its water from wells, and the city system, which drew its water from the Grand River, supplied the citizens of Grand Rapids until 1919. In that year the city purchased the Hydraulic Company. In 1938, after years of discussion and with Works Progress Administration help, the city ran a pipeline from Lake Michigan to Grand Rapids. The lake has been the source of city water ever since.

West Leonard Street, March, 1904.

The Grand River overflowed its banks from time to time, often causing extensive property damage and inconvenience to residents and businesses located nearby. Over the years the city dredged, and built dams and retaining walls, until the river was under better control. Although an occasional flood still creates problems, the "great flood" of March, 1904, was the last that caused major destruction.

Like so many other later public services, charity began at home. Each family was expected to take care of itself. The settlers, however, realized almost from the beginning that certain kinds of economic and social distress must be handled collectively by the community. The preferred method was voluntary contributions through private organizations, but the government on the local level was also involved in public welfare from the very earliest days of village life. In 1916, when a new city charter was adopted, the old "poor office" was changed to the Department of Public Welfare and its responsibilities were expanded to include many different services to those in need.

The public welfare facilities of Grand Rapids were sorely tried by the Great Depression of the 1930's. To meet the desperate needs of the great number of unemployed, the City Manager, George Welsh, with the support of the City Commission, created a public works program with local funds. In addition, the city scrounged food and other necessities from every possible source, and from the record it appears that people were generous although the times were hard.

Those who were put to work on public projects were paid in scrip which was redeemable for food, fuel, and merchandise at municipal stores set up for the purpose. The public works projects were many and varied and were well documented photographically, as the collage of pictures on the next two pages illustrates.

Grand Rapids, Mich., Work Voucher No. C 76930
GOOD FOR ONE DOLLAR $(1.00)
in Groceries, Fuel or Merchandise at City Store
$1.00
NOT TRANSFERABLE
VOID AFTER 60 DAYS

Grand Rapids, Mich., Work Voucher No. D 1[illegible]2885
GOOD FOR TWENTY CENTS (20c)
in Groceries, Fuel or Merchandise at City Store
20¢
NOT TRANSFERABLE
VOID AFTER 60 DAYS

Grading the banks, sewage disposal plant beautification project.

Preparing the road for paving, sewage disposal plant.

Repairing old clothes to be sold for scrip.

Laying the water main on Hall Street.

Cutting and stacking wood from city lots to be sold for scrip.

Laying pipelines.

Canning vegetables and fruit to be sold for scrip.

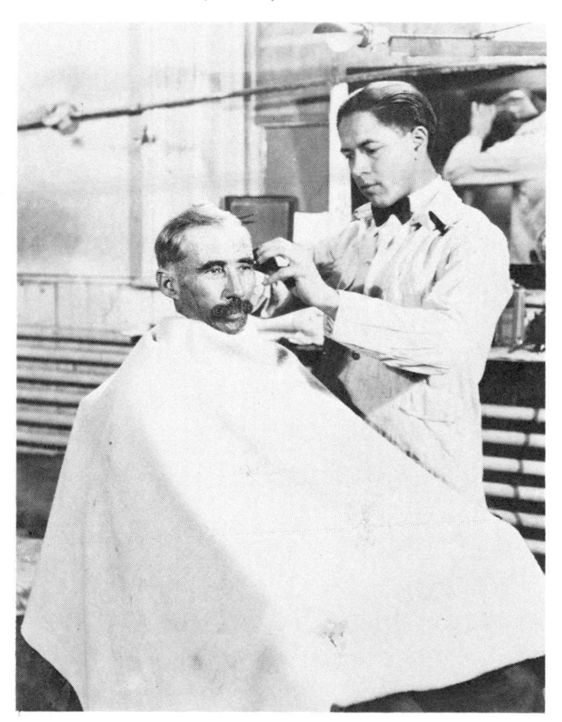

Performing services such as shoe repair and haircutting for other unemployed workers.

Cleaning steel sewer forms.

One of the most controversial projects presided over by George Welsh was the City Social Center for homeless and jobless single men. Some felt that its clients should be contracted out to the Salvation Army. It did, nevertheless, provide a vital service for those most hard-pressed by the depression. The photographs below, taken at the Social Center, include the main room where the men dined and slept, the tiny kitchen where the huge meals were prepared, the storeroom, and the reading room where the men could try to forget their troubles for awhile.

Waiting in line at a municipal grocery store.

Shoe department at a municipal scrip store.

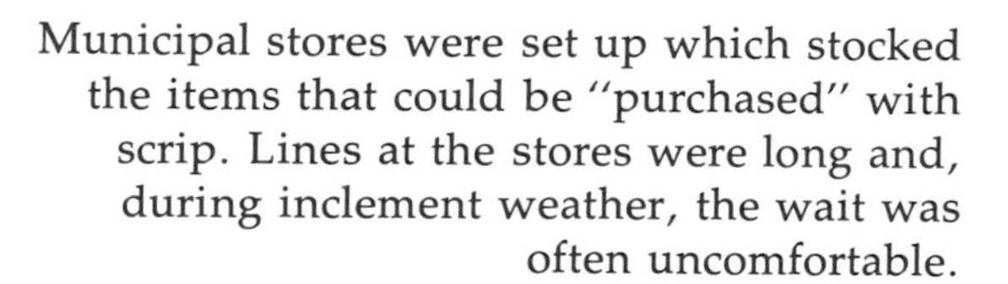

Municipal stores were set up which stocked the items that could be "purchased" with scrip. Lines at the stores were long and, during inclement weather, the wait was often uncomfortable.

Direct relief activities of the city included distribution of milk, bread and potatoes to destitute families. The relief budget of Grand Rapids increased in the first two years of the depression from $65,000 to $1,000,000. The need was great, and the city rose to the challenge.

As the depression dragged on, state and national governments increasingly took over the burden of relief. Grand Rapids can be proud that it had its own Franklin D. Roosevelt in George Welsh and a "little New Deal" two years before the national government acted to meet the needs of its citizens.

Distributing free milk and bread.

Loading potatoes for free distribution.

While the bulk of medical care has remained in the private sector, city and county governments have been actively involved in various aspects of public health. Serious health problems, such as typhoid and tuberculosis, have been successfully combatted by government actions such as improving the sewer systems and legislating the pasteurization of milk. Public health clinics have also been important. A clinic set up in 1915, pictured above, under the Department of Public Health, provided advice and medical care for pregnant women and newborn and young children; it was very effective in reducing the number of deaths of both mothers and their children.

Sunshine Hospital developed from experiments in open-air treatments for tuberculosis patients. In 1907 a fund-raising drive by the Grand Rapids Anti-Tuberculosis Society resulted in the first municipally-owned TB sanitorium in the country. This led to Sunshine Hospital in 1923, which Kent County took over in 1941. With the decline in tuberculosis patients, Sunshine Hospital, called Kent Community today, now cares for chronic disease patients. Kent Oaks, the second public hospital, resulted from a drive to keep people with psychiatric problems out of jail and in a hospital setting. Originally city-owned, Kent Oaks became a function of the county by 1918 and provided a place for those awaiting admission to state hospitals. Today Kent Oaks provides short-term intensive care and outpatient supportive care for ex-patients.

Sunshine Hospital.

An early hospital ward.

Blodgett Memorial Medical Center had its beginnings in 1847 when some local church women formed an association to care for people in need. Reincorporated as the Union Benevolent Association in 1873, the group opened a home and hospital on Bostwick Avenue (top photograph at left) for the aged, infirm, sick and needy. Out of this effort came a hospital, opened in 1886 on College Avenue (bottom photograph at left). In 1916, largely through the work and financial backing of John W. Blodgett, President of the Union Benevolent Association for over twenty-five years, Blodgett Hospital was erected at its present location at Plymouth and Wealthy, S.E.

Butterworth Hospital, originally St. Mark's, built in 1899.

The history of Butterworth Hospital dates back to 1873 when members of St. Mark's Church purchased a frame house on Bond near Crescent for sick and elderly members of the congregation. This was later incorporated as St. Mark's Home and Hospital. In 1887, Richard Butterworth gave money and land at Bostwick and Michigan and, in 1889, St. Mark's Hospital, in the photograph above, was built. The structure which was opened in 1925 and is still in use today resulted from a fund-raising drive along with a gift from Mr. and Mrs. Edward Lowe.

In the late 1800's the family of Mary McNamara deeded her house at 145 Lafayette to Bishop Richter for a hospital (see small photograph at left). The Sisters of Mercy of Big Rapids sent three nursing sisters to Grand Rapids and St. Mary's Hospital was born. Incorporated in 1901 the hospital acquired several adjacent properties and gradually grew into the large contemporary facility that exists today.

Groundbreaking for St. Mary's Hospital addition, 1924.

The first public school in Grand Rapids was opened in 1837. Union-Central (above), one of the larger early schools, was erected at Lyon and Ransom in 1849 with an exterior of Grand River limestone. A tuition of $1.65 was charged for eleven weeks of regular instruction and $2.50 for Greek, Latin, or French studies. The two-story stone schoolhouse below was completed in 1855 on the west side between Broadway and Turner, later the site of Union High School.

Primary School No. 2, in the 1869 photograph above, housed all eight primary grades in two rooms. A new Central High School (below) was completed at Lyon and Barclay in 1868. A year later, in 1869, all public schools became free schools. The public schools were gradually consolidated into a single entity under the control of the municipal government. In 1906 the Board of Education became an independent political entity. In addition to the public schools, Grand Rapids has many parochial Catholic schools and private Christian schools.

Plainfield Avenue School.

Throughout the nineteenth and into the twentieth century, Grand Rapids schools remained fairly small in size.

Straight Street School.

North Ionia School.

As the years passed, large high schools with many diversified services became the norm. Union, Catholic Central, and South, three of Grand Rapids' modern high schools,were all built in the first two decades of the twentieth century.

Union High School.

Catholic Central High School.

South High School.

Palmer School.

Grade schools, however, remained smaller and maintained closer neighborhood ties.

Grandville Avenue Christian School.

By the end of the first quarter of the twentieth century, there were many institutions of higher learning in and near Grand Rapids. In 1914, for example, the Board of Education decided to offer two-year college courses at Central High School, a step which led directly to the development of Grand Rapids Junior College. Even before the turn of the century, however, a variety of opportunities for higher education were available in Grand Rapids. A commercial college was located in the Luce Block on the southwest corner of Monroe and Ottawa by 1865.

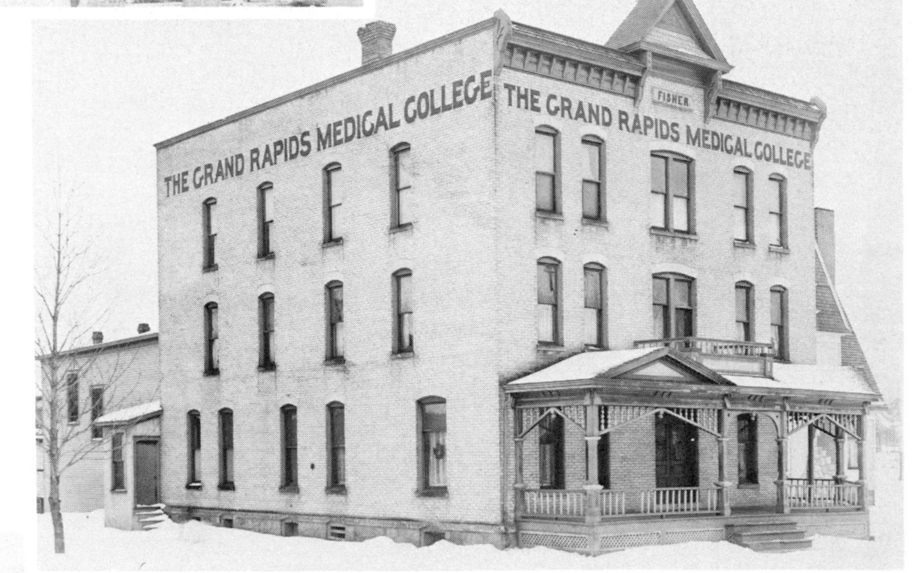

The Grand Rapids Medical College was opened in 1897 by a group of local physicians and eventually graduated 108 medical students. However, the need for more elaborate and formal education for physicians had become evident by the turn of the century and, lacking the funds to develop such a program in Grand Rapids, the medical college closed in 1906.

One of Grand Rapids' early educational institutions that still exists today is the Calvin Theological Seminary. The seminary, with a history dating back to 1876, preceded the development of Calvin College by more than forty years.

The pictures on this and the next three pages illustrate life in the elementary and high schools of Grand Rapids.

Grade school studies in the basics of reading, writing, and arithmetic were broken up with singing, naps, and the like.

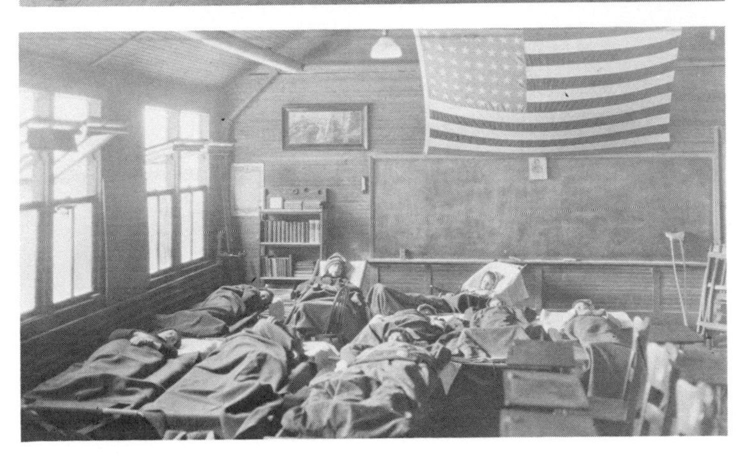

Classroom projects, such as the one resulting in the elaborate display on health care above, were fun. For many, however, recess was always the most enjoyable time spent at school.

In high school studying became a more serious matter, with frequent exams in a variety of subjects, science labs in biology and chemistry, and study halls in which a student was expected to be hard at work.

High schools developed increasingly more diversified curricula. In addition to the traditional academic subjects, vocational training and special interest courses, in fields such as music, were expanded. Physical education was considered an equally important complement to academic learning. Organized sports were always popular and sports programs grew rapidly through the years.

Leonard Crockery.

Libraries, like so many other city services, began as private, volunteer efforts. The deeply religious early settlers came with at least one book in their baggage, the Bible. As any expansion of a private library was costly and useful to only one family, civic leaders began to consider the possibility of a cooperative library. The first of these, containing three hundred volumes, was established by the Grand Rapids Lyceum Association founded in 1843.

The nucleus of the Grand Rapids public library system was formed in 1861 when a district Board of Education came into possession of 855 volumes from the Grand Rapids Library Association. With quarters on the second floor of the Leonard Crockery Store, the Grand Rapids Public Library soon contained 4,045 volumes. In 1875 the library moved to the new Ledyard Building on the corner of Pearl and Ottawa. In 1888 the library was moved once again, this time to the second floor of the City Hall.

The library was finally settled into a home of its own when, in 1901, Martin A. Ryerson, a wealthy Chicago industrialist who had been born in Grand Rapids, donated the amount of $150,000 to construct a new building. The new Ryerson Library was dedicated in 1904.

Ledyard Building.

Second floor, old City Hall.

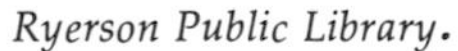

Ryerson Public Library.

Martin A. Ryerson.

Secretarial Office, Ryerson Public Library.

Lobby of Ryerson Library, 1950's.

The new library soon became a great source of pride for the citizens as the number of volumes expanded rapidly. The 1950's photograph of the lobby at Ryerson Library proves it to have been a busy place. To the right are the doors to the Boys and Girls Room where many young people enjoyed a quiet afternoon exploring the wide vistas opened by books. A new 3.2 million dollar addition, begun in 1966, has certainly enlarged and improved the facilities of the public library, but the almost temple-like atmosphere of the old library is missed by many.

West side branch of the public library.

By 1908 the Board of Library Commissioners, concerned with the question of providing better service to all the city's residents, had opened a branch on the west side. Today branches of the library serve the citizens in many sections of the city.

Exhibit at the Kent Scientific Museum, about 1904, includes a long-time favorite of museum visitors, the humpback whale skeleton.

Frank S. DuMond, Director of the Museum for three decades, with visiting schoolchildren, 1928.

Grand Rapids Public Museum, 1920's.

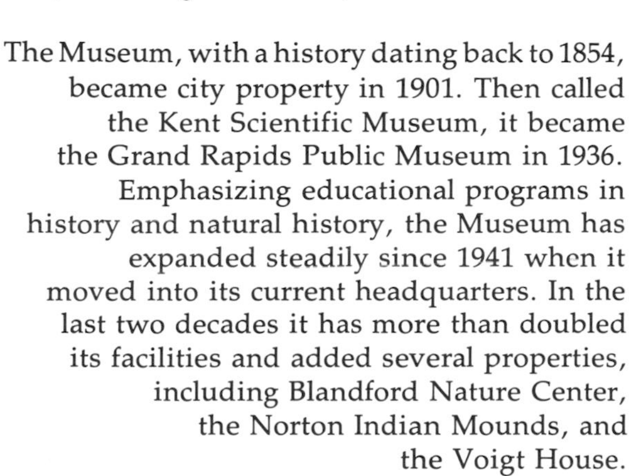

The Museum, with a history dating back to 1854, became city property in 1901. Then called the Kent Scientific Museum, it became the Grand Rapids Public Museum in 1936. Emphasizing educational programs in history and natural history, the Museum has expanded steadily since 1941 when it moved into its current headquarters. In the last two decades it has more than doubled its facilities and added several properties, including Blandford Nature Center, the Norton Indian Mounds, and the Voigt House.

Grand Rapids Public Museum today.

Federal Building, built in 1879.

City Hall, built in 1888.

The city's first Federal Building, constructed in 1879 on Ionia between Pearl and Lyon, housed the post office, federal court, and government offices. A second post office, still standing today although the postal service has moved to larger, modern quarters, was built on the same site in 1909.

The old Gothic-style City Hall on Lyon between Ottawa and Ionia was completed in September, 1888, at a total cost of about $315,000. After considerable controversy, it was torn down in the urban renewal project of the 1960's.

The cornerstone of the old County Building was laid July 4, 1889. Located on the southwest corner of Ottawa and Crescent, it suffered the same fate as the City Hall.

County Building, built in 1889.

For many years these buildings were the center of political and governmental activities in the Grand Rapids area. Out of the urban renewal efforts of the 1960's arose a new multi-million dollar administrative complex of which the citizens can be proud. Still there are those who miss the old City Hall clock which chimed out the hours for all those years.

Over the years the citizens of Grand Rapids campaigned avidly for their favorite candidates in local, state, and national elections. These campaign photographs were taken in Grand Rapids in the presidential election year of 1928 when Al Smith, Democrat, opposed Herbert Hoover, Republican. The Republicans triumphed in the 1928 elections; those from Grand Rapids were particularly pleased with the election of Arthur Vandenberg as United States Senator from Michigan.

Arthur H. Vandenberg, born and raised in Grand Rapids and publisher of the *Grand Rapids Herald,* was first appointed to the Senate by Governor Fred Green upon the death, in 1928, of Senator Ferris of Big Rapids. Elected to the senatorial post later the same year, Vandenberg began a career that lasted for twenty-three years.

Senator Vandenberg achieved national and international prominence as a statesman, and was often mentioned as a possible presidential candidate. After many years as a staunch nationalist and isolationist, he reversed his stand and, in 1945, was appointed by President Franklin D. Roosevelt to help organize the United Nations. In 1946 he was a delegate to the Paris Peace Conference; in 1947 he became president pro tem of the Senate. Vandenberg died of cancer in 1951.

Arthur H. Vandenberg.

Suddenly Grand Rapids is internationally known as the hometown of Gerald R. Ford, 38th President of the United States.

An avid sportsman, Jerry Ford was captain of the football team at the University of Michigan, from which he graduated with honors. After earning his law degree from Yale, Ford was associated with the law firm of Butterfield, Amberg, Law and Buchen prior to his career in public office. In World War II, Ford served with distinction in the United States Navy.

In 1948 Ford was elected to the U.S. House of Representatives from Michigan's Fifth District, a position to which he was reelected twelve times. An able politician, held in high esteem by his colleagues, Jerry Ford was chosen as minority leader of the House in 1965. In 1973 he was nominated by President Nixon, confirmed by the Senate, and installed as the 40th Vice-President. On August 9, 1974, following the resignation of President Richard Nixon, Gerald R. Ford took the oath of office and assumed the Presidency.

President Gerald R. Ford.

Jerry Ford, returning to Grand Rapids as the newly sworn-in President of the United States, is greeted by a hometown crowd. At the podium, Lyman S. Parks, Grand Rapids' first black mayor, has just presented President Ford with a replica of the Calder. Just behind Ford, at the far right, Governor William G. Milliken watches the proceedings.

Paving Company

Workers and Industry

Industrial life in Grand Rapids, typified and led by the furniture industry, has exhibited the diversity and fluctuations of a large urban center. While much of the 19th century urban economy served the needs of local customers, the furniture industry, logging companies, and firms such as the Bissell Company began reaching out to national and international markets. Its department stores, banks, transportation services and wholesale businesses made Grand Rapids an important hub of the regional economy of western Michigan. Transplanted Easterners, French Canadians, Irish, Southern Blacks, Germans, Polish and Dutch, among others, formed the diversified work force. By the early 20th century many of the artisans and skilled laborers of an earlier era found themselves replaced by workers who wore white collars or performed the often monotonous tasks on the assembly lines of the modern factory.

Lumbering and sawmills were among the first major industries in Grand Rapids. The Grand River provided a highway for the logs, power for the mills, and a central location for industrial development. The 1860's and 1870's saw the construction of numerous mills, most powered by steam, that processed the logs as well as the finished lumber needed by the burgeoning city. Pictured above around 1880 from right to left are the Quimby Mill, the Withey Mill, the Robinson and Letellier Mill and, in the background near the bridge, the Grand Rapids Chair Company.

Located in close proximity to the large stands of pine in the Grand River basin, the sawmills reached the height of their production during the 1870's and 1880's. The Grand River with its tributaries annually carried over thirty million board feet of lumber to Grand Rapids for its mills, lumberyards, and furniture factories. In addition, large quanitites of newly harvested timber passed through on the way to Grand Haven or Muskegon. At times, as in this view of a logjam precipitated by the 1883 flood, the river itself would turn into a sea of logs.

Sawmills provided lumber for numerous small companies which in turn produced construction materials and furnishings for Grand Rapids homes and businesses. With the completion of canals along the east and west banks (in 1842 and 1867, respectively), the waterpower of the river was effectively harnessed. Boats could dock on either side and local manufacturers quickly became attracted to riverside locations.

Early milling and manufacturing concerns were generally small, employing perhaps ten to thirty workers. It was not uncommon for the owners of these shops to supervise production and to maintain close contact with the employees. Halladay Lumber Company was one of the many small firms competing in the prospering lumber trade.

The strenuous occupation of lumberjack was the choice of numerous Grand Rapids area workingmen in the nineteenth century. Each stage of the lumbering operation involved long hours, hard, sweaty work and extensive periods of separation from family and friends. The harvesting of trees and the hauling of cut logs was often achieved without aid of machine or steam power. By the 1880's steam engines replaced horse-drawn vehicles for long-distance hauls.

The river became the main highway for transporting the logs. Lumberjacks, working with their pike poles, often called peaveys, stacked the logs in temporary dams to await the high water in spring. Once released, the thick flow of logs enabled the men to "walk on the water", separating the logs and maintaining a smooth flow down the river. Just one log caught up on a boulder could cause a backup of logs, which easily resulted in a jam. With swift and accurate use of the pike pole, the men could free the trapped log and prevent a pileup.

The high quality pine and hardwoods available in the nearby forests attracted pioneer furniture makers to Grand Rapids. Originally oriented to the local markets, many of these firms, such as the wicker chair company in the 1890's photograph at left, were small shops employing only a few workers.

Under the leadership of men such as William Haldane, C. C. Comstock, George Gay, William Berkey, and William T. Powers, the furniture industry expanded and larger firms began to emerge. With customers in national and international markets, companies such as Berkey & Gay and Phoenix Furniture expanded their work forces into the hundreds and established Grand Rapids' reputation in the industry. Beginning with simple household necessities such as tables and chairs, the furniture men of Grand Rapids produced large quantities of basic products as well as finer, more exquisite furnishings.

Berkey & Gay Furniture Company

Phoenix Furniture Company

The Widdicomb Furniture Company, 1870's.

The Widdicomb Furniture Company, as did many early firms that prospered, expanded into a large, complex operation that nestled closely among neighboring houses. Over 700 men and women found employment here during the depression years of the 1870's.

Work began early at the lumberyards and drying kilns of the John Widdicomb plant in the 1930's. St. Adalbert's Catholic Church stands majestically in close proximity to its industrial neighbor as the early morning fog begins to rise.

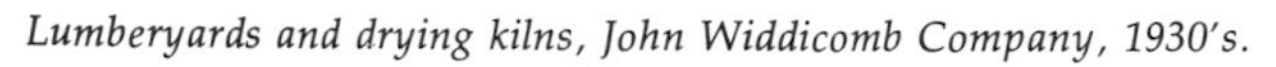

Lumberyards and drying kilns, John Widdicomb Company, 1930's.

Woodcarvers at a local furniture factory.

Furniture decorating department, Berkey & Gay.

The tradition of the skilled artisan was a potent force in the Grand Rapids' furniture industry. Working at his individual bench with tools worn to fit his hands, the woodcarver practiced his trade in a pre-industrial fashion. Complementing the woodcarver, the varnisher and painter of quality furniture engaged in a different set of artistic skills.

Although the furniture industry attracted large numbers of skilled woodworkers and decorators, many of the semi-skilled and unskilled, both male and female, found jobs in the burgeoning industry. By 1910 the introduction of various machines began to shift more emphasis to modern technological methods. One of the issues in the momentous furniture strike of 1911 was the introduction of piecework systems that seemed to threaten the artisan's sense of workmanship.

Young worker toils at a power sander.

Lathe department, Widdicomb Furniture Co.

Accounting and stenography department, Steele Furniture Co., 1930's.

In the larger furniture companies, the front office, with its complement of typists, stenographers, bookkeepers, accountants, and office managers, grew apace with expanding factory output.

Furniture made Grand Rapids famous. The initial success of several of the early cabinetmakers drew others to the city who were interested in the design and manufacture of fine furniture. The industry continued to grow in size and reputation until Grand Rapids became known as the Furniture City. Semiannual markets, initiated in the late 1800's, drew thousands of furniture dealers, designers, and interior decorators from throughout the country and from many foreign countries as well. Changing patterns of marketing and distribution inevitably lessened Grand Rapids' predominance in the furniture industry in the last few decades. However, many local companies have maintained national prominence as manufacturers of quality furniture for homes, offices, and schools.

Furniture manufacturing coexisted in Grand Rapids with a great variety of other industries. By the 1860's and 1870's, flour milled in Grand Rapids was being shipped to markets throughout the eastern half of the United States. The flour companies eventually succumbed to the increasingly strong competition from wheat and flour producers of the western plains, but local millers enjoyed many decades of success and profit in the meantime.

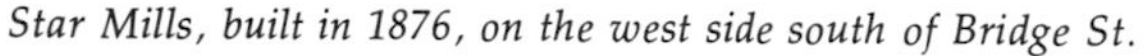

Star Mills, built in 1876, on the west side south of Bridge St.

These early mills utilized a substantial amount of the power of the Grand River. The Valley City Mills, for example, needed about 40% of the waterpower available to the manufacturers on the east side canal.

The Valley City Mills built in 1867.

The Voigt Mill on Pearl Street.

The Voigt Milling Company, founded in the 1880's, produced quality flour for nationwide customers. The old mill on Pearl Street, with its stone foundation arching over the river that had provided its waterpower, had an old world charm that was lost to Grand Rapids when the mill burned down in the 1960's.

The Voigt Milling Co. with its "Crescent" brand and the Valley City Milling Co. marketing "Lily White Flour" were the largest mills in Grand Rapids. There were many smaller mills in the area. The Mill Creek Mills in Plainfield Township was one of the earlier ventures in the industry and, like many of the mid-nineteenth century businesses, it divided its interest between wholesale and retail trade. The retail store was established across the street from the mill.

The Mill Creek Mills. The retail store, third building up the street on the left, was also owned by Plumb & Sons.

G. C. Fitch Co., 1890.

Raymond & Scranton, 1869.

In the 1800's, Grand Rapids industry was dominated by small shops. The G. C. Fitch wagon factory on North Division and the Raymond & Scranton carriage works at Justice and Louis avenues, though small in size, were still larger than this storefront workshop (left) on Ionia near Crescent.

Throughout the late 1800's and early 1900's, business operations tended to increase in size. During the 1890's, the work force of men, women, and boys recruited by the Grand Rapids Felt Boot and Shoe Company was large compared to those of most earlier shoemaking concerns.

The H. M. Reynolds Asphalt Shingle Company was organized on a large scale. The asphalt shingles, introduced by Herbert Reynolds in 1908, offered a measure of fire protection to Grand Rapids homes which had previously been roofed with highly inflammable wooden shake shingles.

Many Grand Rapids industries utilized local resources. Gypsum, found in multiple layers along the banks of the Grand River south of the city, was one of the most important resources and provided decades of profit for local industries. One of these, the Alabastine Company, produced a high-quality, gypsum-base wall covering.

Employees of the Felt Boot and Shoe Company, 1893.

The H. M. Reynolds Asphalt Shingle Company.

The Alabastine Company's plaster mills.

Other local industries were dependent on imports of raw materials. The I. C. Shipman Coal Company (at left, above), located near the residential area around Plainfield and Leonard, was one of these.

In the early 1900's the small carriage factories of an earlier era were gradually replaced by plants manufacturing automobiles and automotive parts. Several cars and trucks were produced in Grand Rapids prior to the depression of the 1930's. One of these, the Austin, an aristocratic touring car with a four cylinder, 50 h.p. engine, was designed and built by a Grand Rapids man, Walter S. Austin. By the end of the depression, Detroit had a firm hold on the manufacture of automobiles which it has never again relinquished. However, the manufacture of automotive parts and supplies in Grand Rapids continued to grow apace with the progress of the industry in Detroit. As early as the late 1920's, the Hayes Body Corporation, making car bodies for Chrysler, Marmon, Reo, and Willys-Overland, had become Grand Rapids' largest employer with over three thousand persons on its payroll.

The 1905 Austin.

Hayes Body Corporation, 1928.

The ordinary household carpet sweeper catapulted one small Grand Rapids firm to fame and fortune. With its rotating brushes and light, compact size, the innovative carpet sweeper threatened to replace spring and fall backyard carpet beatings and to supplement the traditional stick-handled broom. Originally a sideline to the crockery and glassware business of Bissell and Sons, the first sweepers were assembled on the third floor above the store. Melville Bissell, the inventor of the carpet sweeper, is on the far right in this photograph.

Within ten years after patenting his improved sweeper in 1876, Bissell relocated in newly constructed buildings on Mill Street (above). As early as 1885, he utilized a staff of seven traveling salesmen (right) in order to penetrate distant markets, cope with vigorous competition, and try to change the habits of broom-oriented customers. By 1893, Bissell was producing one thousand carpet sweepers a day.

Christopher Kusterer's brewery.

The brewery industry provides an interesting example of the changing trends in production and distribution that occurred in the century between 1850 and 1950. Established in 1847, Christopher Kusterer's lager beer was the product of one of the earliest breweries in Grand Rapids. His small group of workmen regularly filled the large barrels in the background and sold their fermented contents on the local market.

Petersen Brewing Company.

By the 1890's a number of large and medium-sized firms emerged, such as the Grand Rapids Brewing Company and the Petersen Brewing Company (renamed the West Side Brewery after prohibition).

Local temperance advocates surely disapproved of the increasing flow of "Silver Foam" in the local saloons and taverns. Whether sold by the bucket or the bottle, good locally produced lager and pilsner beers were a popular refreshment for many a thirsty worker or businessman. After the repeal of prohibition, national advertising and distribution networks enabled Milwaukee and St. Louis beers to begin to displace the local brews.

The Grand Rapids branch of the Blatz Company was the entering wedge that led to the eventual demise of the locally produced beers. In 1951, Fox Deluxe, Grand Rapids' last local beer, followed the others out of business.

Before the era of the chain store, wholesale dealers in drugs, dry goods, notions, hardware, produce, and groceries were vital links in the Grand Rapids economy. Acting as intermediaries between cities and between city and countryside, wholesalers helped stock the crowded shelves of the neighborhood stores in Grand Rapids. Before the advent of the refrigerated railroad car, a large portion of local meat supplies came from the wholesale butcher shop in the photograph above.

Abe Schefman & Company (below) carried a full line of vegetables and fruit. Many of these commodities were shipped from local farms, such as those in Hudsonville and Newaygo, as well as from more distant areas.

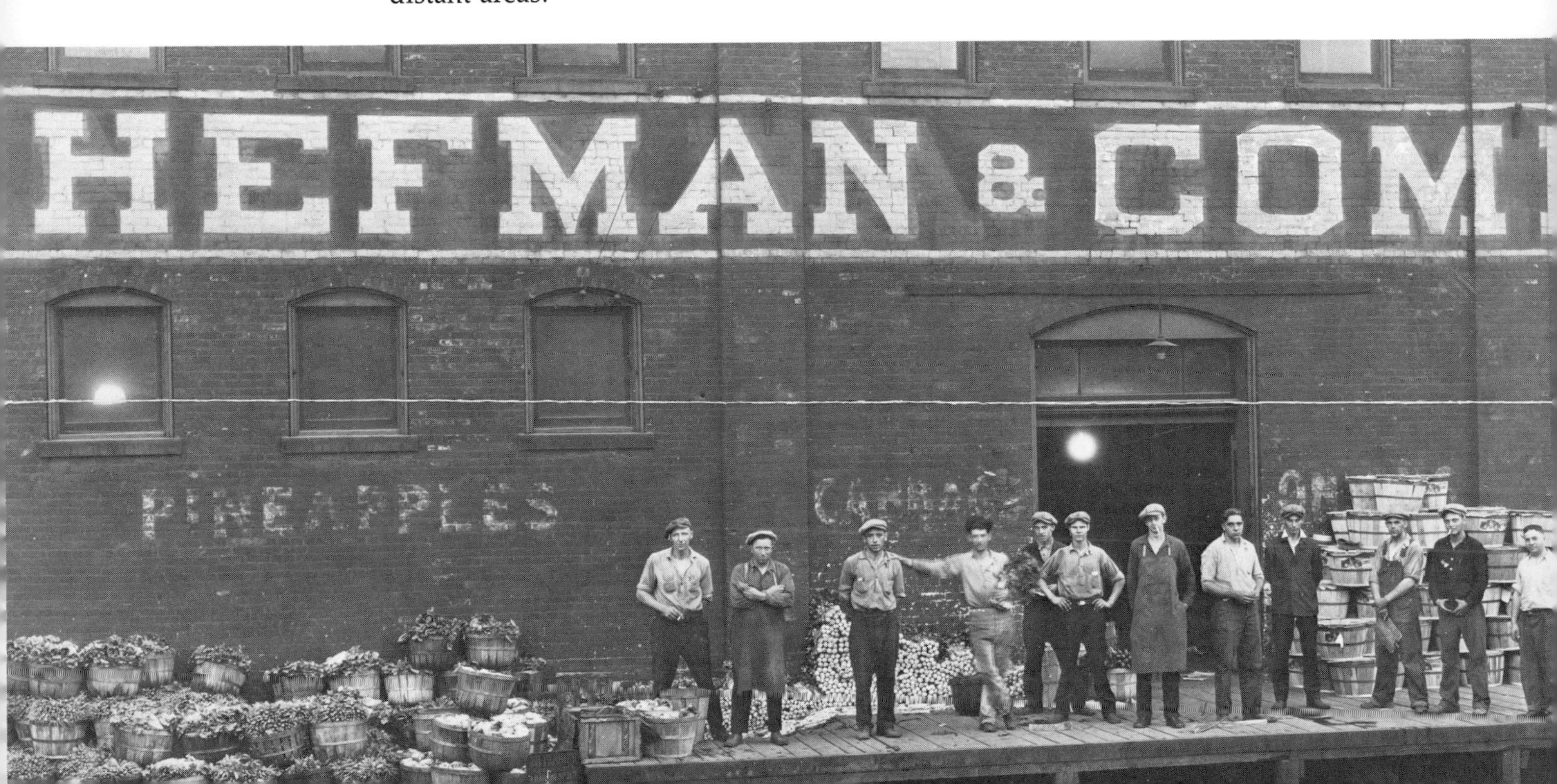

Shields, Bulkley, & Lemon, 13-19 S. Division, 1883.

Perhaps the most important of the wholesalers was the grocer who distributed a wide variety of household food items. Both city markets and more distant village and country general stores were dependent on companies such as Shields, Bulkley, & Lemon. This firm seems to be doing a fair business with the teamsters loading their wagons at the side entrance and dozens of barrels, some perhaps holding crackers or pickles, ready to be shipped out.

1876 Centennial decorations adorn this building at the southwest corner of Monroe and Ionia, today the site of the Michigan National Bank Building. In the 1870's, however, Horton & Stewart, retail grocers, occupied the main floor of this building. The basement was occupied by F. VanDriele & Company, "wholesale and retail dealers in flour, feed and grain."

58 Monroe, about 1885.

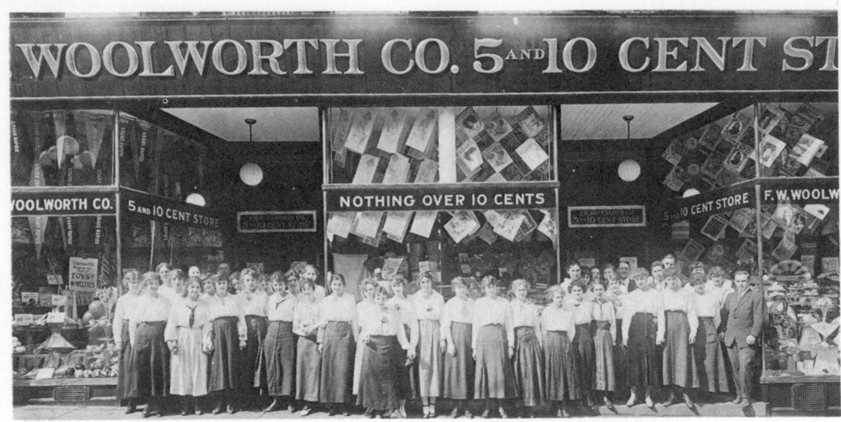

Woolworth's 5 & 10 Cent Store.

As Grand Rapids grew in size, the number and variety of firms dealing in retail goods and services increased rapidly. Many workers found employment in one or another of these operations. At 58 Monroe, around 1885, L. D. Putnam, Druggist, occupied the storefront at street level. Upstairs, J. D. Jennings provided custom tailoring and "society supplies and regalias", while W. L. Dickenson operated an employment agency, in those days called an "intelligence office". Some early concerns were just beginning a long history. F. W. Woolworth Company, whose national chain of five-and-ten-cent stores was a new idea in marketing when the Grand Rapids store opened in 1912, is still in business today on Monroe near Campau Square. Shellman Optical Company has been in operation continuously since 1891 on Monroe near Ottawa. Ryskamp Brothers, selling paints, wallpapers, and other home decorating supplies, opened in the 500 block of Eastern, S.E., in 1892 and remained in business there until 1974.

Shellman Optical Company.

Ryskamp Brothers.

Large manufacturing concerns, in addition to furniture and automotive supply companies, proliferated as the city grew, employing thousands of local workers. These included, to name only a few of the many which had early beginnings in Grand Rapids, Oliver Machinery, Keeler and Wolverine brass companies, and American Box Board. Leonard Refrigerator, which introduced "a better icebox" in 1881, later became part of Kelvinator.

Leonard Refrigerator Company.

The Dean-Hicks Company.

Printing and publishing became major industries in Grand Rapids. The city became a center for religious publication with Eerdman and Zondervan publishing houses leading the way. Dean-Hicks Company, one of many important printing concerns in the city, opened shop in Grand Rapids as Dean Printing in 1883.

The Fine Arts (Exhibitors) Building under construction, 1920's.

Additional diversity in the local economy came from public and private construction projects which provided jobs for large numbers of skilled and unskilled workers.

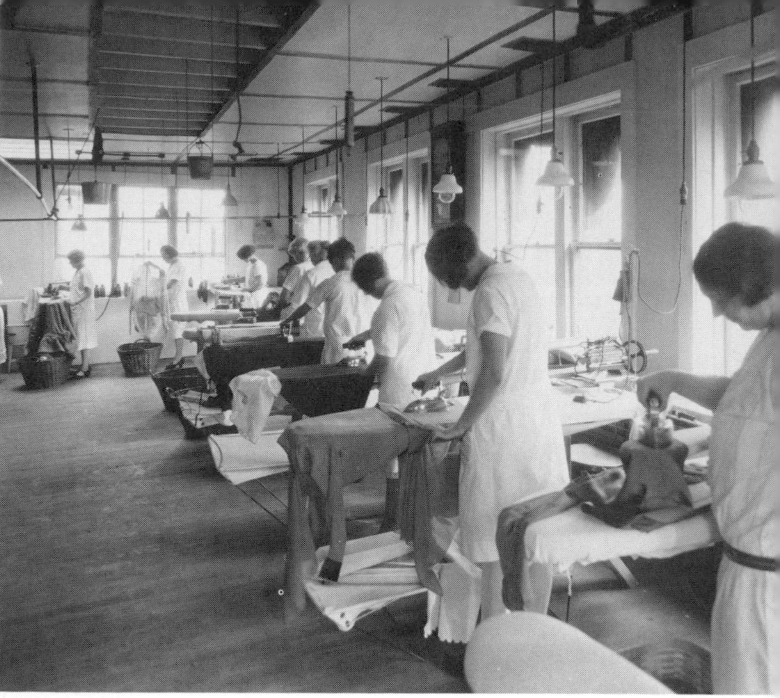

Employment opportunities for women increased in the 1900's. Some of these were traditionally "woman's work"; numerous women were hired as seamstresses and in laundries. Jobs in which manual dexterity was important, such as cigar making, a major Grand Rapids industry around the turn of the century, were often open to women (see photograph, bottom left). The two World Wars, during which many young men were unavailable for local employment, brought many women into occupations that had formerly been reserved for men.

Hotels and restaurants employed a diversified work force. Substantial numbers of black workers found employment in downtown restaurants and hotels, as is apparent in the picture above of the Pantlind Hotel staff in the 1940's.

Both male and female workers found the newly developed opportunities in white-collar work to their liking. The 1920's photograph below of a secretarial school illustrates this increasingly viable alternative to traditional factory work. Many chose this type of training and employment as Grand Rapids emerged as a regional center in the economy of western Michigan.

When not working, employees of Grand Rapids firms found time for other activities. A noon-hour baseball game with male and female participants on the roof of Globe Knitting Works (above) provides a contrast to the employees leaving for lunch outside the Wolverine Brass Company (right). The employees of a local dry cleaning establishment take a break from work to display a new purchase, the latest design in fire extinguishers (below).

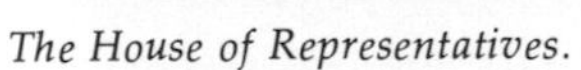

The House of Representatives.

The Senate.

The Cabinet, American Seating Company, 1920's.

An interesting experiment in dealing with labor/management problems was developed by the American Seating Company in the early 1900's as an alternative to unionization and employer paternalism. The rank and file employees elected one representative for every forty workers. This House of Representatives, as it was called, was complemented by a Senate composed of the foremen and department heads. At the apex of the structure were the vice-presidents and administrative chiefs who formed the Cabinet.

A more common form of labor organization was the traditional union whose members often marched in the Labor Day parades along Monroe Avenue. Local harness makers (Grand Rapids chapter, United Brotherhood of Leather Workers on Horse Goods) posed for the photograph at right on Labor Day, about 1912.

A contingent of the harness makers union.

Much of the history of industrial development in Grand Rapids is revealed in this 1920's photograph of the Berkey & Gay Furniture Company at its riverside location on the east bank of the Grand River. The belching smokestacks contrast with the neighboring homes of employees and customers, portraying the prosperity of the city and its hopes for the future. With a history tracing back to the mid-1800's and developed with the local resources of wood, waterpower and workmanship, the Berkey & Gay plant and its environs also symbolize the accomplishments of the past.

Modern Expressway

Getting from Here to There

The story of transportation in Grand Rapids encompasses the changes from the one-horse carriage of pre-Civil War days to the family automobile of the 20th century. Steam-powered river boats, stagecoaches, railroads, electrified streetcars, interurbans, buses and airplanes all played an important part. Beginning in the 1850's with the stagecoach, the horse-drawn trolley, and the advent of the passenger train, public transportation systems were dominant for three quarters of a century. Only with the development of the automobile did Grand Rapids, like so many other cities, adopt an essentially private transportation system.

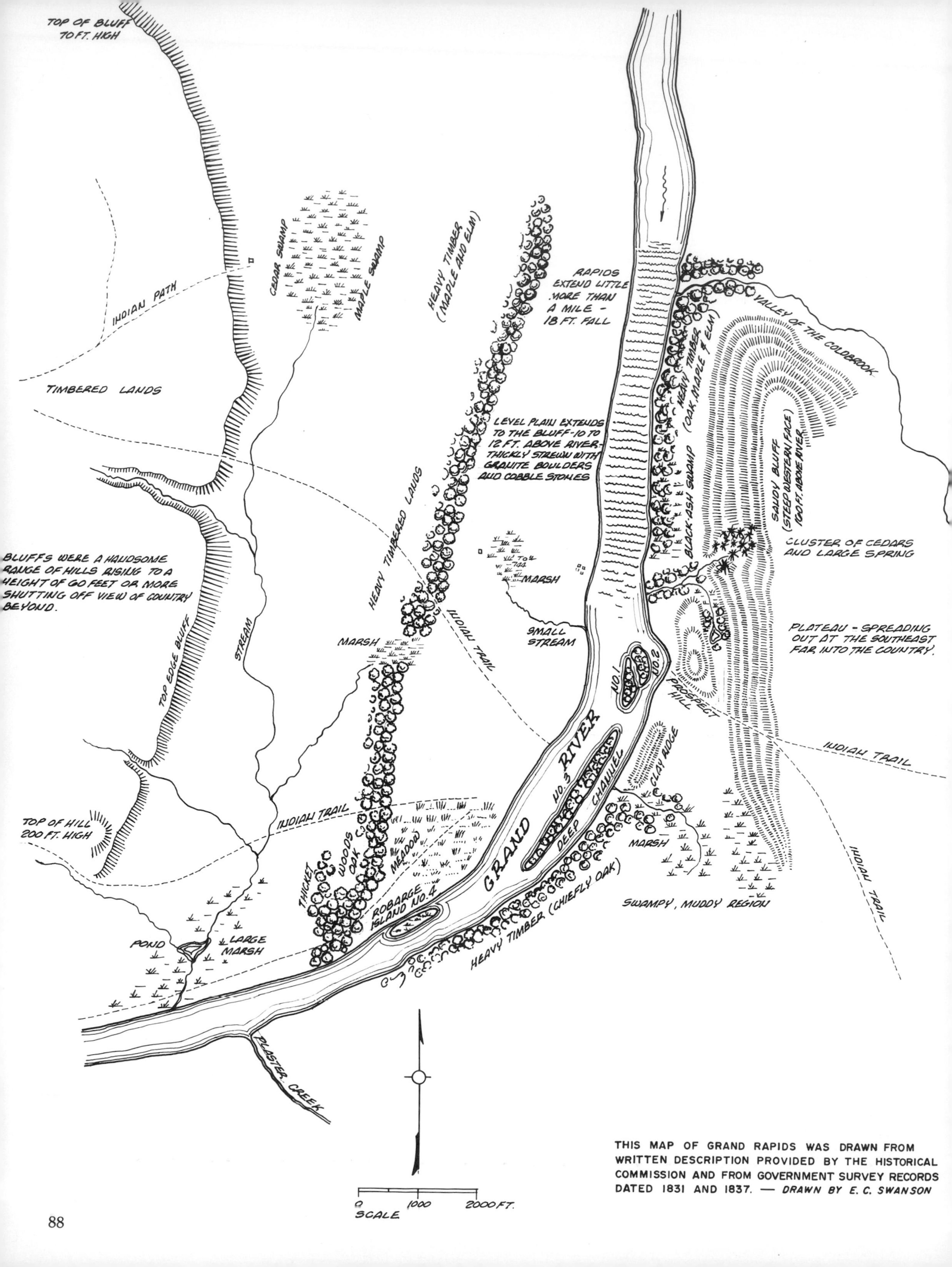

THIS MAP OF GRAND RAPIDS WAS DRAWN FROM WRITTEN DESCRIPTION PROVIDED BY THE HISTORICAL COMMISSION AND FROM GOVERNMENT SURVEY RECORDS DATED 1831 AND 1837. — *DRAWN BY E. C. SWANSON*

Early Grand Rapids highways followed along the paths of preexistent Indian trails (see map on opposite page). Monroe Avenue replaced the southeast trail, while the old Grand Rapids and Walker Plank Road retraced the main western route. Most roads, however, were built on the square, grid layout established in the Northwest Ordinance of 1787. The orderly, methodical quality of these easily surveyed roads (such as Division, Eastern, Leonard, and Bridge) was occasionally broken by roadways with configurations conforming to the rivers, marshes, and hills in the Grand Valley basin.

Poor conditions on these early roads, especially during wet weather, spurred the development of plank and gravel pavings. An 1848 state law required that toll roads must be eighteen-feet wide, with at least nine feet covered by three-inch-thick planks. The law was amended in 1855 to include gravel roads. Eight companies, organized between 1873 and 1886, operated the toll roads indicated on the map below. Along these roads passengers and cargo were conveyed to and from the city limits in all directions.

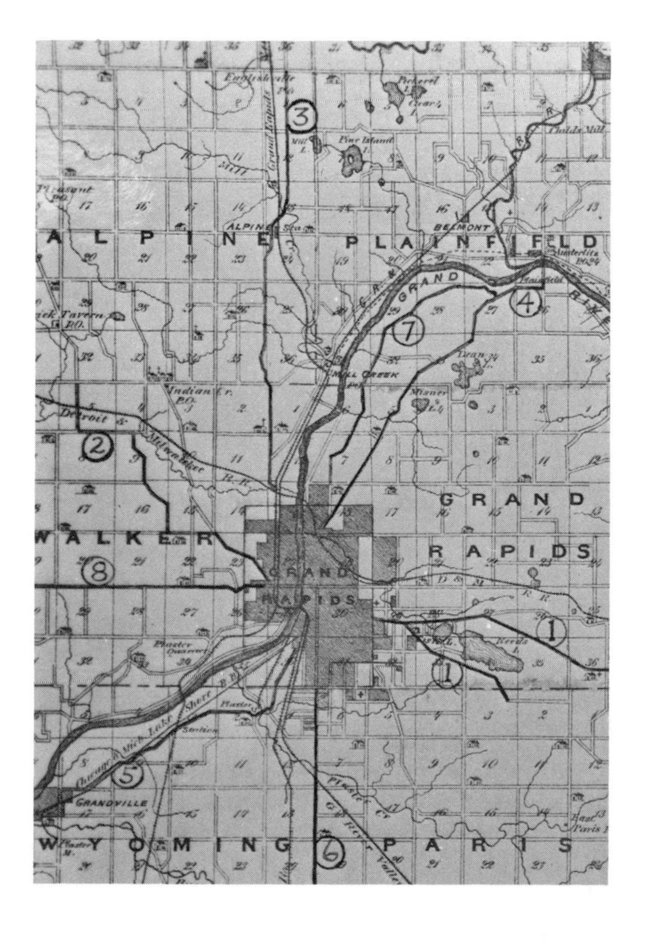

1. *Reeds Lake Avenue Company operated two gravel roads. One started at Eastern Avenue and continued for three miles along Lake Drive to a point south of Reeds Lake. The other ran for five miles from Lake Drive along Robinson Road north of the lake.*
2. *Grand Rapids and Walker Plank Road Company operated an eight-mile-long road in a northwesterly direction out of Grand Rapids to a point on the north line of Walker Township.*
3. *Alpine Plank Road Company maintained a road that traveled north for nine miles to Englishville.*
4. *Plainfield Gravel Road Company's road followed M-131 along Plainfield Avenue for five miles.*
5. *Grandville Plank Road Company developed a five-mile-long road from Hall Street to the city of Grandville.*
6. *The road operated by the Division Avenue Gravel Road Company was the most profitable of the toll roads. It traveled out Division Avenue from Hall Street for nine-and-one-half miles.*
7. *Canal Street Gravel Road Company maintained a road that followed the east side of the river for eight miles along Coit Road from North Park and eventually tied up with the Plainfield toll road.*
8. *West Bridge Street and Allendale Gravel Road Company's road went straight west from Bridge Street for nine miles to a point on the Grand River.*

The William J. Blacklock family operated this tollgate on Robinson Road north of Reeds Lake. State law established a one-cent-per-mile toll for single-horse carriages. Although these roads made travel easier and more comfortable, freight haulers and travelers often found the tolls annoying.

Tolls helped pay for the frequent maintenance required on these early highways. Planks needed replacing and flattening, while gravel roads required a regular rolling to insure safe travel. The Reeds Lake Avenue Company operated this horse-drawn roller that serviced its Robinson Road and Lake Drive routes.

This gathering of neighbors on the Division Avenue toll road between Oakes and Cherry streets shows the raised wooden sidewalks as well as one of the numerous freight wagons that plied the toll roads and streets of Grand Rapids in the nineteenth century.

The F. J. Porter, *1852-1858.*

The L. Jenison, *1867-1875.*

Land travel took a back seat to river transportation in the early years of Grand Rapids. For early settlers migrating to Grand Rapids from points east, trading with Ottawa Indians on one of the river islands, or shipping goods to Grand Haven or Chicago, the river served as the city's first major highway. The *F. J. Porter,* built in 1852 and owned by Grand Rapids' first mayor, Henry Williams, was an upstream side-wheeler during the heyday of steamboats before the railroad era.

The *L. Jenison,* with its shallow draft and powerful steam engine, navigated the upstream waters above the rapids. Eight years after its introduction to river traffic in 1867, the *L. Jenison,* like many other boats, succumbed to the primary danger of that time when it burned to the water line. The Hovey Dock near Fulton Street, pictured here, was only one of many such riverfront facilities in the 1870's.

The west side canal.

The growth of river traffic in the 1840's stimulated interest in the construction of a system of canals and locks around the rapids for navigation through the eighteen-foot water drop between Leonard and Pearl streets. The locks were never completed, however, and the project was abandoned in 1855. Canals were built and widened on the east side in 1842 and on the west side in 1867.

Dams were constructed to direct the flow of water to the canals that supplied the waterpower for riverside factories. A sixteen-foot gap in the Fourth Street dam built in 1866 (above) furnished enough space for rafts of logs to pass over the dam and down the narrow channel in the rapids.

The 130-foot *W. H. Barrett* began its twenty-year career in 1874 primarily as a freighter. Its fourteen-inch draft protected it from sandbars and hidden river obstructions. Later a second deck and comfortable passenger accommodations were added as freight traffic dropped off. A downstream side-wheeler, the *W. H. Barrett* was destroyed by fire in 1894.

The Carrie J.

The Grand.

The river islands below the rapids provided docking and winter storage quarters for Grand River steamboats. The *Carrie J*, shown here in 1900 between islands three and four and the east bank, was a picturesque river freighter with its two side-wheel paddles and somewhat undersized proportions.

The last serious attempt to revive river freight and passenger traffic appeared with sister boats which were given the names *Grand* and *Rapids*. Built in 1905 in Grand Rapids, as were most of the river steamers, these large boats were in use for only two years before being sold at auction.

Logging literally dominated the waters of the Grand River during the 1870's and 1880's. More than two billion board feet of timber arrived at Grand Rapids en route to Muskegon and Grand Haven. Local sawmills and furniture companies consumed nearly 750,000,000 board feet during these two decades. The Grand Rapids Boom Company conducted this sorting operation in front of Long's Sawmill on the west side.

The river was also a temporary barrier between the east and west sides of the city. But fording places, ferries, and sleighs gave way to covered bridges after 1845. Several early bridges, such as those at Bridge, Pearl, and Leonard streets, were built by private companies which collected tolls. Public discontent with the toll system brought results by the years 1873-4 when the city purchased these bridges and converted them to free use. In 1858 the new Pearl Street bridge, despite the tolls, was the talk of the town.

The Pearl Street Bridge, 1858-1885.

The Leonard Street Bridge, 1857-1879.

The covered wooden bridges were built to accomodate both foot passengers and horse-drawn vehicles. Walkways were built along the outer walls of this bridge at Leonard Street to protect pedestrians from the other traffic. The sign on the facade carried the message: "Warning. Five Dollar Fine for Driving Faster Than a Walk." Prior to 1873, a toll collector on the west side of the bridge enforced rates ranging from one cent for foot passengers to four cents for two-horse carriages.

Dismantling Fulton Street Bridge, 1927.

Two generations of bridges followed the era of the covered wood bridge. Wrought iron spans constructed during the late nineteenth century included the heavy-duty trusses required to support streetcars. One such bridge, completed in 1885 at Fulton Street, was torn down in 1927 with plenty of onlookers helping the project along.

By the 1910's new methods of construction provided wide concrete arches supported by a steel skeleton. Costs had risen dramatically since the day of the wooden bridge. While the first bridge at Pearl Street cost $16,000 in 1858, a high price at the time, the 1922 span, though nearly fifty feet shorter, cost almost a quarter of a million dollars.

Pearl Street Bridge, completed in 1922.

Leonard Street Bridge, completed in 1913.

A coach of the Good Intent Line, at the Plainwell rest stop, 1865.

As early as 1836, when Grand Rapids was a village of only five hundred residents, three stagecoaches per week pulled in from points south. Road travel took a big step forward in 1885 with the completion of a plank road between Grand Rapids and Kalamazoo where travelers could make connection with the Michigan Central Railroad. During the 1860's as many as eight stagecoaches daily made the run between the two cities, carrying mail, light cargo, and passengers such as the Civil War veterans in the photograph above. Stage lines were not to be needed much longer, however, for railroad service was rapidly expanding.

A locomotive engine of the GR&I Railroad at the platform of the first Union Station.

The Detroit and Milwaukee Railroad began service to Grand Rapids in 1858; twelve years later, with railroad traffic to and from the city rapidly increasing, the first Union Station was constructed. The Grand Rapids and Indiana Railroad, with its southerly connection to Kalamazoo and points south, complemented and competed with the Detroit and Milwaukee operation.

The Chicago and West Michigan Railway aided in the extension of direct service from Grand Rapids to the markets of Chicago. This 1880's railroad crew worked out of the depot at Holland. The locomotive was a wood burner and the large, screen-covered smokestack aided in trapping hot cinders and preventing fires.

During the 1870's mail and express service, here combined with the first car of a mid-1870's run between Lansing and Grand Rapids, complemented the regular freight and passenger service. The tree stumps in the foreground give evidence of the vast natural resources of wood for construction which were readily available to the railroad companies.

Larger and more powerful locomotives were common on most routes by 1900. Pere Marquette Engine No. 394 stands on the Fourth Street turntable in Grand Rapids.

The railroads brought weekend shoppers and family outings to Grand Rapids. The Grand Rapids and Indiana Railroad, by then a part of the Pennsylvania Railroad system, reported over two thousand such passengers from southern Michigan on a warm weekend in October, 1900. The platform at Union Station was often crowded when these trains arrived or departed.

The growth of Grand Rapids and its railroad traffic justified the construction in 1900 of a new Union Station along with a train shed to shield passengers from the elements. With this new depot, its six pairs of tracks, two wide walkways, and convenient downtown location, Grand Rapids' railroad development had reached its zenith. Sixty-one years later the depot was razed for an interstate highway right of way.

Two very different aspects of railroad experience are recorded in these pictures. Perhaps many Grand Rapidians still remember arriving home late in the evening and passing familiar landmarks on the last stage of a journey from Big Rapids, Chicago, or Detroit. Occasionally, passengers traveling to or from Grand Rapids experienced a train wreck. Fortunately, few of these were as dramatic as the head-on collision below.

Canal Street, looking north from Campau Square, 1870.

Monroe Avenue, looking west towards Campau Square, 1876.

City transportation in the 1860's and 1870's depended largely upon horse power. Looking north from Campau Square, Canal Street (now Lower Monroe) is filled with carriages and freight wagons, including a well-loaded wagon of hay on the left and a horse-drawn streetcar waiting at the switch. On Monroe Avenue the weekday routine appears busier than normal amid the 1876 Centennial decorations.

The era of the horse-drawn vehicle lasted for nearly three quarters of a century. While passenger traffic shifted to electric streetcars in the 1890's, the hauling and carting business continued to use horses into the second decade of the twentieth century. These teamsters, as the drivers were called, often worked for small companies or, in some cases, owned their individual rigs.

The man standing on the wagon was not only the driver but the unloader and shoveler of his load of coal. At the turn of the century his was a familiar face on the streets and in the neighborhoods of Grand Rapids.

The end of one era and the beginning of another are visible in the 1910's picture of the Security Storage and Transfer Company at 47 Market Avenue. The teamster on the right seems to be making a symbolic yet real departure behind his two white horses, while the trucker on the left appears ready and willing to take over.

Early streetcars were also propelled by horse power. The transportation needs of a city with over ten thousand residents spurred the development of a number of streetcar lines in the post-Civil War period. At the peak of the era of horse-drawn transportation, the network of public transit lines covered nearly forty miles in Grand Rapids.

In 1885 the owners of the streetcar line running from downtown Grand Rapids to the amusement center at Reeds Lake replaced the horse-drawn cars with "dummy" steam engines. Despite the protests of residents along the route, these noisy and dirty engines remained in use until the 1890's when electrified cars took over.

The hills east of downtown Grand Rapids made a full streetcar too heavy for horses to pull. In 1888, the Valley City Street and Cable Company introduced cable cars, modeled on the San Francisco system, to the hill district. Although residents of the area had looked forward with enthusiasm to the cable car system, a million-dollar capital investment, disappointing revenues, broken cables, and labor conflicts plagued the company, and the venture was short-lived.

Looking north down Canal Street (now Lower Monroe) from Campau Square, about 1890.

Strong competition emerged between the various transit companies of the city, with the result that they often operated at a loss. Another consequence of the rivalry between the owners of the streetcar lines was unnecessary duplication, obvious in the above photograph of Canal Street where four sets of tracks had been constructed. The existing transit companies were merged into the Consolidated Street Railway Company in 1890 as a system of monopoly replaced competition in mass transportation. Soon after the merger, all streetcars in the Grand Rapids system had been electrified.

Looking west across Bridge Street Bridge, around the turn of the century.

Accommodations on the streetcars of the early 1900's were comfortable by the standards of the day. The seats could be folded back for a foursome, advertisements provided distractions as did a company publication called the *Trolley Tropics*, lights and ventilation proved adequate, and windows could be opened on a balmy day. The *Grand Rapids Herald* was also available for purchase by the passenger.

All of this, however, probably counted for very little in the eyes of these youngsters who may have been bound for the amusements at Ramona Park when this Cherry Street car was derailed.

Lafayette Avenue, near Delaware.

West Fulton Street.

Before the advent of the automobile, streetcars nearly monopolized passenger traffic in the city. Most areas of the city had convenient, efficient service to downtown shopping and entertainment, and most streetcar lines were oriented toward the downtown district. A residential street, such as Lafayette Avenue (above left), nearly empty and unpaved, was dominated by the presence of the early twentieth-century streetcar. Local merchants along the streetcar routes, such as West Fulton Street (above right), relied on the customers conveyed by an effective mass transportation system.

The streetcar system reached its peak of development in the early 1920's with over seventy miles of streetcar lines. Passenger traffic, however, had declined from a total of thirty million passengers in 1915 to only twenty-three million in 1923.

In 1925 Grand Rapids had just purchased a new fleet of modern streetcars, consequence of a 1924 fire which had destroyed nearly half of the other trolleys. Yet looking up Monroe Avenue from Campau Sq., the rapidly emerging competition of the private automobile is evident.

Interurban tracks, at left, spanned the Grand River just north of Pearl St. Bridge.

Misfortune interrupts service on the interurban line through Jenison.

Auto-urban bus serving Grand Rapids, Rockford, Greenville, and Lakeview.

The popularity of the electric trolley for urban mass transit encouraged businessmen to develop the interurban electric railway system. Traveling at speeds up to fifty and sixty miles per hour, these mini-trains provided quick, frequent, and efficient service to Muskegon, Holland, Kalamazoo and numerous closer communities. Weekend excursions to the beaches at Holland and Saugatuck were available on the route that traveled through Jenison, at times with unhappy results.

Buses and auto-urbans began to compete with the railroads and interurban trolleys in the 1920's. With greater mobility and lower operating costs, these gasoline-fueled vehicles forced the heavily capitalized interurbans out of business by 1929, less than thirty years after they were constructed.

The North Star Lines with its modern, efficient and attractive buses emerged as an important cog in Grand Rapids' transportation system. During the depression year of 1930, North Star added these buses to its growing fleet.

As early as 1923 buses were integrated into the mass transit system. This Alpine Avenue bus began the "feeder" system—the bus line connected up with an electric trolley line on W. Leonard Street. Originally intended as a supplement to existing trolleys, bus service gradually expanded until it began to replace streetcar lines in the early 1930's.

An extensive street-widening project, begun during the late 1920's and expanded during the depression years of the 1930's, hastened the eventual demise of the trolleys. On Division Avenue (below), as on other streets, the rails and ties were removed and, upon the resurfacing of the street, buses reigned where once the streetcar was king. By 1935, Grand Rapids was an all-bus city.

Division Avenue at Fulton Street, 1928.

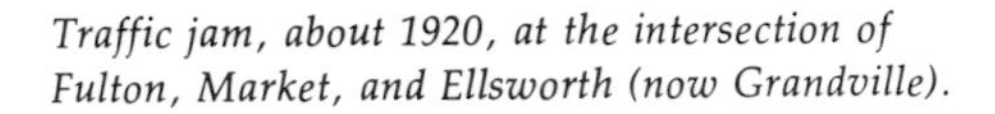

Traffic jam, about 1920, at the intersection of Fulton, Market, and Ellsworth (now Grandville).

Lauferski's Auto Livery, a converted horse barn.

Parking lots and used car lots began to proliferate.

The 1920's witnessed the widespread introduction of the automobile into urban transportation. In its wake came such new urban phenomena as traffic jams, parking lots, and gasoline stations.

The corner gas station became a familiar sight.

The automobile had a major impact on public transportation systems. Railroads, streetcars and, later, buses all experienced a decline in passengers as more and more people began to rely on the privately owned car. The interurbans became a thing of the past.

Red Top Cab Stand at Union Station.

Automobile accidents gave rise to a new business, the towing service.

City officials welcome a new air service to Grand Rapids.

The airplane came to Grand Rapids in the 1910's. Roseswift Airplane Company began freight and passenger service to and from Grand Rapids in 1919. The early air services utilized the fields of an old work farm at the south end of Madison Avenue, the site that became the first Grand Rapids airport.

Grand opening, Grand Rapids Airport, 1926.

The new airport opened officially in July, 1926. An enthusiastic crowd of 40,000 watched a demonstration by the Detroit-Grand Rapids Airline, one of the first companies to provide regular service to Grand Rapids. Air travel, the latest development in transportation, was here to stay.

Kohler amphibian landing Milwaukee passengers in Grand Rapids, 1930.

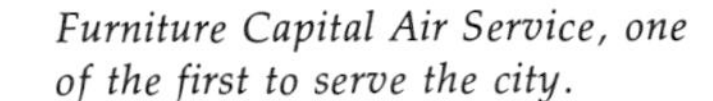

Furniture Capital Air Service, one of the first to serve the city.

Immanuel Lutheran Church

Churches and Organizations

Religious institutions have played an important role in the development of Grand Rapids. From the very outset, Catholics mingled with and built their churches among the more numerous Baptist, Methodist, Congregational, Lutheran, Reformed and other Protestant denominations. Smaller in number, but equally important in the history of the city, were the congregations of the Jewish faith. Churches and church-sponsored organizations were complemented by a large number of fraternal, cultural and charitable groups. Although more numerous and perhaps more significant around the turn of the century before their social functions were partially supplanted by the impact of modern media, service and social organizations expanded the influence of the individual citizen on the society at large.

Catholic church built by Louis Campau, 1837.

Churches were among the most significant private institutions in the social life of Grand Rapids. Although for the members of each congregation, their own church, large or small, was of primary importance, certain faiths were decidedly more influential in the religious life of the city. Among these one must note Baptist, Catholic, Christian Reformed, Reformed, Methodist, Congregational, Episcopal, Presbyterian, and Lutheran.

As in numerous Michigan communities, the early French settlers brought the Catholic faith to Grand Rapids. City founder, Louis Campau, had this church constructed at the corner of Monroe and Division in 1837; but the church was never turned over to the Catholics. Embroiled in a long-standing conflict with the local priest, Fr. Viszosky, Campau sold the church in 1841 to the Congregationalists. The Catholics constructed their first permanent church, St. Andrew's, in 1850.

Reformed congregations established their presence in the city in the 1840's as the first in a long line of Dutch settlers arrived in Grand Rapids. As with other groups of settlers, one of their first responsibilities was to build an appropriate, if modest, house of worship. The members of the congregation of the First Reformed Church had come west from the long-established Dutch communities in and around New York. A few years later Dutch-speaking immigrants from the Netherlands organized the Second Reformed Church. Eventually the two congregations united to become the Central Reformed Church.

First Reformed Church, built in 1842.

St. Mark's Episcopal Church at Crescent & Division, built in 1840.

St. Mark's Episcopal Church was housed in this modest frame structure with a capacity of 170 persons. As with many other early churches, the building was sold to a different denomination, in this case the Baptists, when a larger congregation and increased prosperity enabled the Episcopalians to move to a more commodious structure.

St. Mark's Church.

Limestone from the riverbed of the Grand River provided the construction materials for the second St. Mark's Church which still stands on Division Avenue between Lyon and Fountain. When completed in the early 1850's, the sedate, small town character of Grand Rapids was still much in evidence.

Twenty years later, in 1872, this view of Bostwick Avenue, in a residential district on the outskirts of downtown Grand Rapids, illustrates the increasingly urban character of the city. Impressive church edifices were part of that growth. Fountain Street Baptist Church, on the far left, towers above its neighbors in a stately fashion indicating quite a growth from the early Baptist mission on the shores of the Grand River. The First Methodist Church (then called Methodist Episcopal), on the corner of Fountain and Division, was equally impressive; a decade earlier the Methodists had only a circuit-riding preacher who came to town once a month.

View of Grand Rapids, 1872, with Bostwick Avenue in the foreground.

A substantial growth in the Catholic population in the last two decades of the nineteenth century produced two new churches, increasing the Catholic total to seven parishes. St. Adalbert's was organized in 1881 on the west side in close proximity to companies, such as the John Widdicomb furniture company, where many of the Polish communicants worked. St. Isidore's laid its cornerstone in 1897 in the Polish neighborhood that was rapidly expanding in the northwest section of the city.

St. Adalbert's Catholic Church, 1930.

St. Isidore's Catholic Church, 1931.

Wealthy Street Baptist Church.

Franklin Street Christian Reformed Church.

The churches of Grand Rapids were organized in response to the growing mobility of the urban population of the twentieth-century city. Downtown churches remained important. The Baptists built their expansive Wealthy Street church for a congregation that lived throughout the various city neighborhoods. Franklin Street Christian Reformed Church, with its imposing dome and columns, was considerably larger than earlier churches built by members of this denomination. Immanuel Lutheran Church has served its members from the same location at the corner of Michigan and North Division since 1856.

Immanuel Lutheran Church.

Second Congregational Church.

Grace Episcopal Church.

Scribner St. Baptist Church.

Neighborhood churches, however, remained an integral part of the city's religious life. Nestled in among the numerous houses of Grand Rapids' developing neighborhoods, Scribner Street Baptist Church, Grace Episcopal Church, and Second Congregational Church reflected the continued vitality of the Protestant groups.

Griggs St. Evangelical Church.

Many members of the congregation of the Griggs Street Evangelical United Brethren Church, organized in 1907, were active in mission work. The Evangelical Church in Grand Rapids dates back to 1881.

Temple Ahavas Achim.

The first Jewish settlers in Grand Rapids, followers of liberal Judaism, organized religious services in the 1850's; this group later became the congregation of Temple Emanuel. Conservative Judaism came later with the founding of the synagogue Temple Beth Israel in 1898. Ahavas Achim, the second conservative congregation, was organized in 1911.

The two wedding photographs below illustrate both the continued growth of Black churches in Grand Rapids, dating back to the African Methodist Episcopal churches of the nineteenth century, and the growing diversity of religious practices in the community, including the Eastern Orthodox churches which were new to Grand Rapids in the early twentieth century.

Elks band at B.P.O.E. headquarters, corner of Ottawa and Lyon.

Grand Rapids has followed the general rule that America is a nation made up of joiners. Many organizations, dedicated to a diversity of goals, have been important to the city.

In the early years of the 1900's, fraternal groups became extremely popular. They provided a social club atmosphere for their members and mutual protection from unforeseen economic crises, offering low-cost insurance providing accident and death benefits when few other agencies did so. The various community services financed by these groups were of enormous value to the city.

The Benevolent and Protective Order of Elks, founded in 1886, was one of the first fraternal orders in Grand Rapids that still exists today. The name of the organization illustrates its purpose. The Elks performed many charitable services for the community, providing, for example, new shoes for two thousand impoverished young people in 1915. Another fraternal organization that flourished nationwide during the early twentieth century was the Woodmen of the World. Members of Maple Camp No. 33, the Grand Rapids chapter of the Woodmen, posed for the photograph below.

As early as 1844 the Grand Lodge, Free and Accepted Masons, was in existence in Grand Rapids. The Shriners Band, pictured here, is just one of many activities of this order.

The Knights of Columbus, a Roman Catholic fraternal organization, provided a number of essential social services financed in part through volunteer efforts.

Free evening school, conducted by the Knights of Columbus, for ex-servicemen returning from World War I.

Other Grand Rapids fraternal groups included the Moose, the Odd Fellows, the Maccabees, the Order of Owls, and the Fraternal Neighbors.
All of them provided their members with a feeling of belonging, a sense of caring and being cared about. If you needed help, social or economic, you could always count on your brothers.

The Kiwanis Club of Grand Rapids was formed in 1916 with one hundred charter members. The group sponsored an impressive list of community action programs that included financial help for Mary Free Bed Hospital and the Junior Achievement Program, as well as many other organizations. In this picture the Kiwanis Clubs of Michigan are providing logistical support and direction for a youth band.

In 1919 the Lions Club was officially welcomed to the roster of clubs in the city. Like the Kiwanis, it was dedicated to the task of making the city a better place in which to live. Whenever the Lions International held a convention in the city, as they did in 1934, Grand Rapidians were sure to turn out in force to watch their parades and to help the festivities along by decorating the central business district with flags and colorful banners.

Various organizations often cooperated to achieve their goals. In the 1930's photograph at right the Lions Club joined the Salvation Army in raising money to buy Christmas baskets for the city's poor.

The Peninsular Club was organized in 1881 as a private association for the wealthy and the prominent of the city. This building on Ottawa Avenue and Fountain Street was the tasteful clubhouse of the Peninsular Club from 1883 to 1914. The present structure on the site was completed in 1914 and remodeled many times since then.

The Peninsular Club.

To serve the down and out a group of concerned citizens organized the City Mission at Market Avenue and Louis Street. One year later, in 1900, Mel Trotter came from Chicago to begin his long association with the mission. In fact, he became its driving force through his preaching services, revival meetings, and crusades to rescue the destitute from the "demon rum".

The women of Grand Rapids were also active organizers. One women's group of the 1920's was the Daughters of America which emphasized civic and patriotic duties.

Women's suffrage campaign headquarters, 1912.

The Grand Rapids chapter of the national American Women's Suffrage Association helped in gaining the vote for women in Michigan in 1918, two years before the national amendment was adopted.

After women gained that right, members of the League of Women Voters became active in voter registration drives, in efforts to "get out the vote", and in general discussions of political issues.

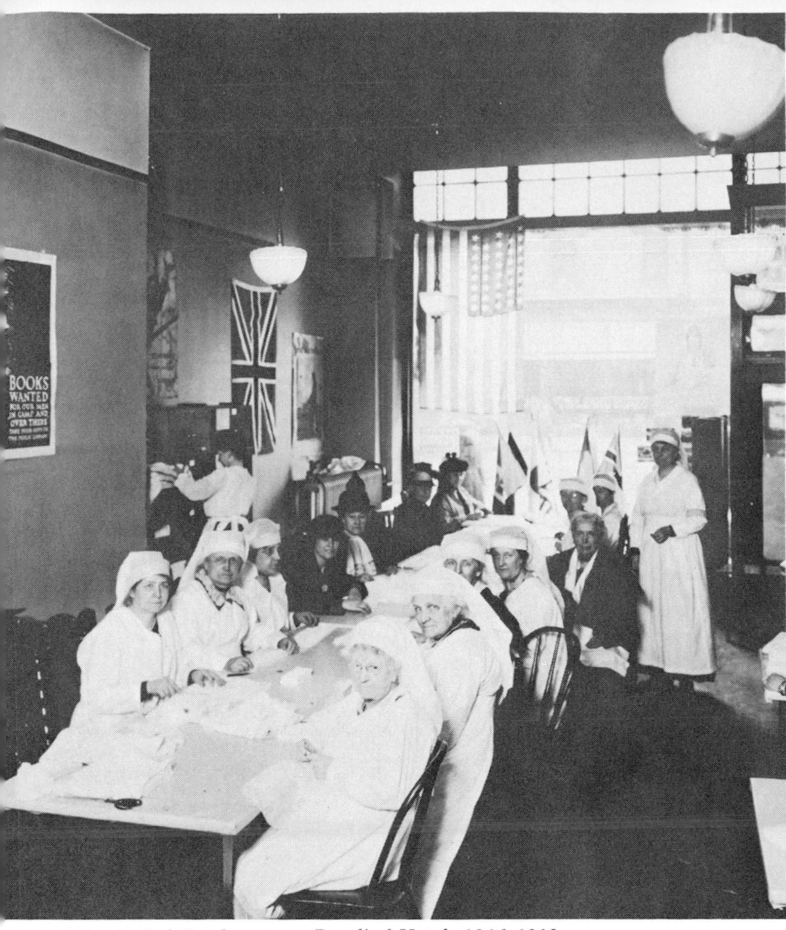

War Relief Headquarters, Pantlind Hotel, 1916-1919.

Grand Rapids Anti-Tuberculosis Society, 1927.

The women of the city have always been active in charitable causes. Volunteer efforts engaged numerous local women at the War Relief Headquarters (above left) during World War I. Many volunteers work each year in campaigns to raise funds to help solve national health problems; the 1927 photograph (above right) was taken to promote the sale of Christmas Seals. The Santa Claus Girls, whose goal is to provide Christmas gifts for all children of the community who otherwise might not receive any, has been a popular community program since 1908.

Santa Claus Girls, 1928.

Ladies Literary Club.

Interests in literature, art and music were supported and promoted by a variety of community organizations, usually initiated by the local women.

Reading and study clubs were important to the early settlers and established a tradition that did not disappear as other entertainments became available. Many literary clubs, including the three illustrated here, have been established in the city over the years.

West Side Ladies Literary Club.

Annual dinner dance of the Lincoln Literary Club, February 12, 1930.

The Grand Rapids Art Museum.

The fine arts were given impetus by the formation of the Grand Rapids Art Association in the early 1900's. In 1920 Mrs. Emily J. Clark offered the Association the historic Pike House on Fulton Street East. This 1844 building, with an addition in the rear, still houses the collections of the Grand Rapids Art Museum and, each year, a variety of visiting art shows can be seen in its galleries. Classes in various art forms are offered by the museum.

Much of the finest music enjoyed by the residents of Grand Rapids for almost a century has been made possible through the dedication of members of the St. Cecilia Music Society. The goal of the society, founded in 1883 by nine local women, is "to promote the study and appreciation of music in all its branches; and to encourage the development of music in the community". In the auditorium of the St. Cecilia Music Building, renowned for its accoustical excellence, the community has enjoyed performances by some of the world's most famous musical artists. Another organization important to the city's music lovers is the Grand Rapids Symphony Society, founded in 1929; the efforts of the members of this society through the years have sustained an increasingly excellent symphonic orchestra of which the community can be proud.

Auditorium, St. Cecilia Music Building built in 1894.

An early St. Cecilia Chorus.

The YMCA about 1900.

Grand Rapids was fortunate in having a Young Men's Christian Association (YMCA) located in the city by 1866. At first operating out of the First Congregational Church, the YMCA offered evening classes and lecture courses as well as physical education. Later expanded to include camping activities and industrial programs, the YMCA was housed in the structure on Lyon at Ionia that is now called the Federal Square Building (left). The main YMCA building on Library Street today was built in 1914.

The Young Women's Christian Association (YWCA), founded in 1900, used rented facilities for almost a quarter of a century. Finally in 1921 a building was constructed on Sheldon Avenue to house the YWCA. With the new facilities, the services were also expanded to include an adult education program, Camp Newaygo, and a residence hall for local and visiting women.

Laying the cornerstone for the new YWCA, 1921.

Boy Scouts advertising the 1927 Christmas Seal campaign.

Not only were men and women organized into clubs, but also the children. In 1910 Henry Eyer, Secretary of the YMCA Boy's Department, stimulated a citizen's committee to establish a Boy Scout organization. After two years of planning, the Grand Valley Council of the Boy Scouts was instituted to provide young males a healthful and invigorating life experience. It not only stressed camping and the outdoor life, but also the cultivation of the ideal of community service. At about the same time, organizations with similar programs were developed for the girls. The Camp Fire Girls, organized by the YWCA, came into existence in Grand Rapids in 1912, followed by the Girl Scouts in 1914.

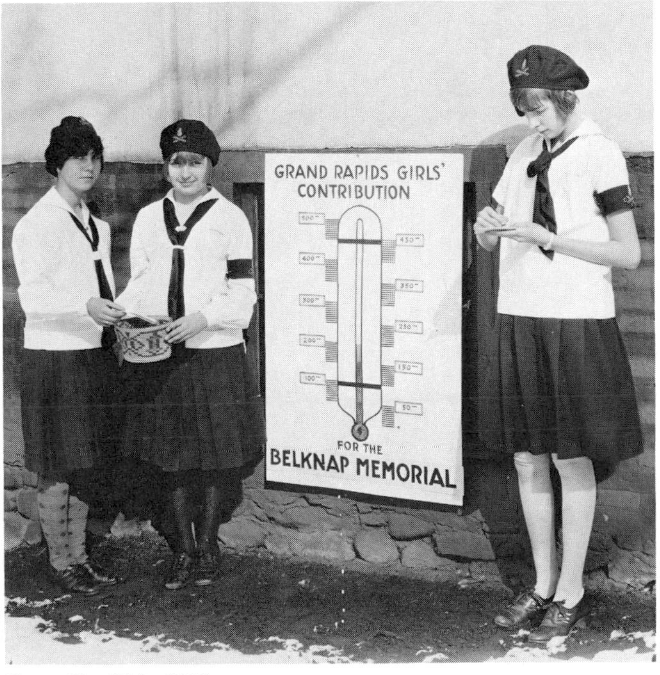

Camp Fire Girls, 1929.

Americanization class, American Seating Company.

Confronted with heavy foreign immigration around the turn of the century, several city groups, such as the YMCA, the Americanization Council, and the Board of Education, fashioned programs to help these newcomers. Classes were set up that taught the immigrants how to speak, read, and write English, how to become citizens of the United States, and how to cope with their new life styles in American society. Occasionally the programs were overly zealous, causing the immigrants to lose faith in their own culture. Nevertheless, the men in these pictures, some attending night school after having worked hard all day, apparently felt that it was well worth the extra effort to attend the classes.

Citizenship class, evening school at Union High.

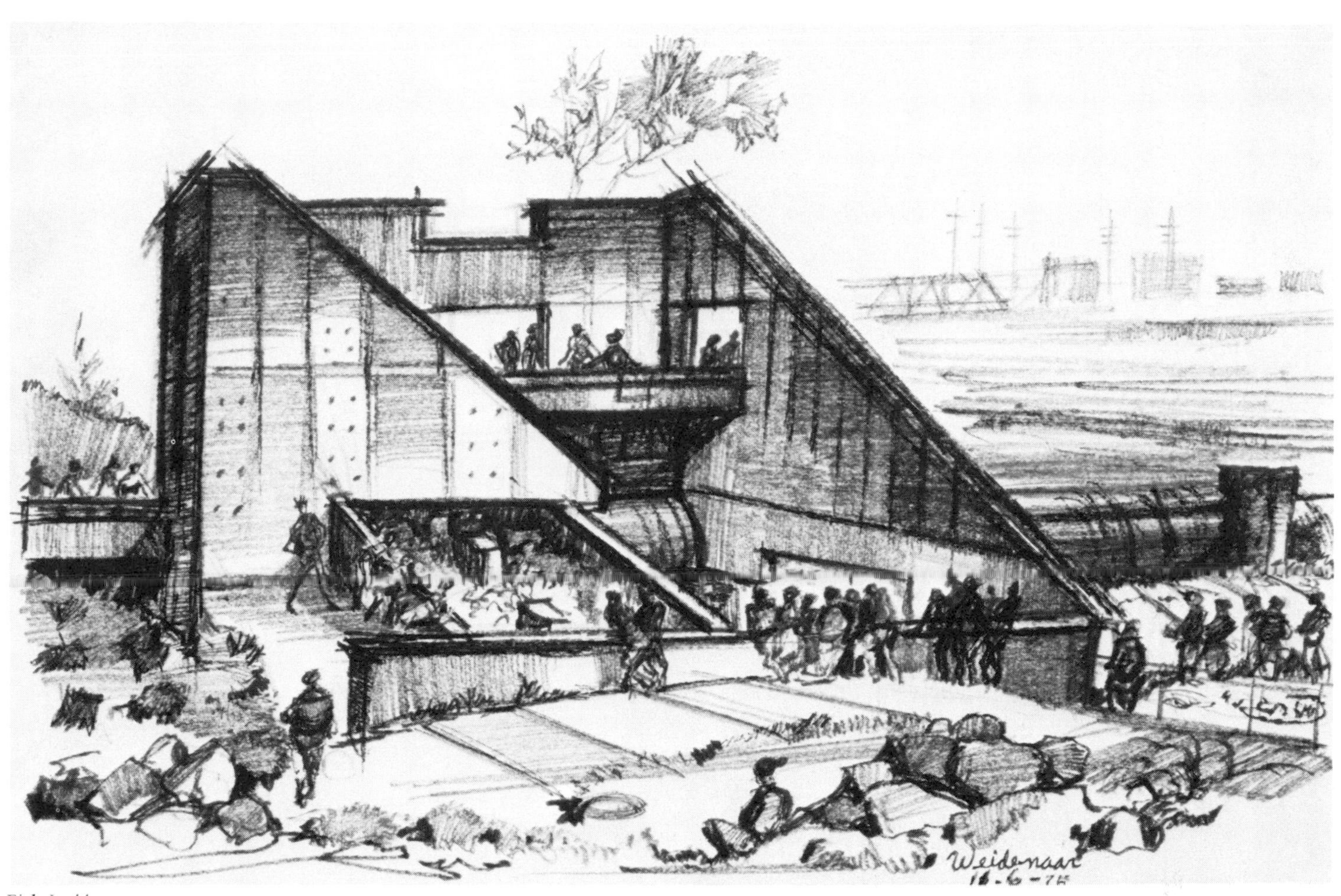

Fish Ladder

Leisure and Entertainment

The early settlers of Grand Rapids, perhaps to dispel the loneliness of the open country, got together frequently for long hours of visiting, feasting, and dancing in each others homes. Gatherings of friends and neighbors to help in raising a house or barn or harvesting a crop meant a day of arduous work followed by an evening of merriment. In village days, there were church sociables and school exercises to attend, as well as philosophical or political debates and temperance meetings for those so inclined. Grand Rapids grew rapidly into a good-sized community and from early in its history has been able to provide its citizens with ample opportunities to enjoy themselves.

Entrance to John Ball Park, 1900.

A favorite activity on a warm summer afternoon was to visit one of the tree-shaded parks of the city. There one could stroll through the park, sit on a bench to read, meet friends and neighbors, eat a picnic lunch, or take a short nap.

Covered spring in John Ball Park, a favorite gathering place on a hot summer day.

Swimming pond at John Ball Park.

One of Grand Rapids' most frequented recreation areas was John Ball Park. In 1884 the pioneer, John Ball, bequeathed to the city forty wooded, hilly acres located on the outskirts of town. These acres, and adjoining land purchased later, were developed into an attractive park including a picnic area high on a hill overlooking the city, a zoo, a pond, a greenhouse, a bandshell and dance pavilion.

Interior of John Ball Park around the turn of the century.

To honor John Ball for his generosity, the city voted in 1924 to establish a monument to his memory. The sculpture of John Ball, with his great-grandson, John Ball III, and his great-granddaughter, Virginia Ball, was unveiled near the entrance to the park in 1925. Standing next to the statue is its creator, the noted New York sculptor, Pompeo Coppini. From the beginning, the statue has been a "living figure" with children crawling over and playing on it—the statue seems to invite another child to sit on its lap.

On warm, sunny days men and women from the stuffy offices, factories, and stores of downtown Grand Rapids would stroll over to Fulton Park (now Veterans' Memorial Park). Many enjoyed eating their lunch at the noon hour in the deep cool shade of the trees. In the restful calm of the park, shoppers stopped to rest tired feet; mothers and nursemaids pushed baby carriages or sat to watch their young children at play; elderly and retired men gathered to share thoughts and memories; and, no doubt, idlers lingered to wile away part of the long, empty day.

Fulton Park in the early 1900's.

Fulton Park in the early 1900's.

The land that became Fulton Park was donated to the county in the 1830's. The county maintained a courthouse there until the early 1850's when it abandoned the site and the land became a city park. In the early settlement days there was little need for public recreation areas in the city as everyone's backyard opened onto the rural countryside. As Grand Rapids grew, more and more people were caught in the endless miles of buildings and streets and needed to escape to the open green space of the parks. By the early 1900's, Fulton Park, the first of these grassy spots, was only one of many city parks.

Original memorial pylons, Veterans' Memorial Park.

In 1926 the City Commission authorized the raising of granite pillars with the names of Grand Rapids' World War I dead inscribed on them. Fulton Park thus became Veterans' Memorial Park. Since 1957 monuments have been added to honor the citizens who lost their lives in subsequent wars.

Band concert, unidentified park.

Swimming pool at Richmond Park.

The city parks provided people with space for many popular activities, such as band concerts, picnics, swimming, and other sports and games.

If a park was not available, an empty sandlot was often nearby and could be used for a community baseball game.

Women's softball team of the American Seating Company.

One of the most attractive areas near Grand Rapids is Reeds Lake. Although it was the site of an 1830's settlement, it was not until near the turn of the century that an entertainment center began to develop along the west shore of the lake. Herbert B. Miller's Boat Livery, which was opened at this location in 1881, rented small boats to men and women who could row out upon the lake to enjoy the gentle breezes and the wild, beautiful scenery along the shore. Next door to Miller's was the home of Captain John H. Poisson and his family, who operated steamboats on the lake beginning in the early 1880's. Across the street, near the intersection of Wealthy Street and Lakeside Drive, was Godfrey's Saloon, the large building with a double-decked porch.

Miller's Boat Livery on the west shore of Reeds Lake.

Reeds Lake steamers, the Hazel A. *and the* Major Watson *(top); the patio of Kruizenga's Refreshment Garden on the west shore of Reeds Lake, July, 1934 (middle); Ramona Park amusement center (bottom).*

For many decades steamboats plied Reeds Lake offering cruises to sightseers and picnickers. Two rival steamboats pictured here, the *Hazel A.* in the foreground and the *Major Watson* behind her, were not lacking for customers on this summer day. The *Hazel A.* operated on the lake from 1894 to 1925, the *Major Watson* from 1891 to 1926.

Visitors to Ramona Park could sit and relax at J. Kruizenga's Refreshment Garden while watching the activities on the lake. Approaching the dock is the *Ramona* which outlived by almost twenty years all the other steamers on the lake. The *Ramona* did not go out of business until the early 1950's and will still be remembered by many residents of the Grand Rapids area.

As the years passed the amusement center grew, spreading out along the west shore of the lake and occupying a large area across the street as well. The attractions included a small steam railroad, a pavilion where nationally known entertainers performed, a boat slide into the lake, a roller coaster and numerous other rides.

Although millions came to Reeds Lake over the years, the automobile and changing tastes caused declining revenues by the mid-1900's. Ramona Park is now the site of a shopping center and apartment complex. On the waterfront where the steamers once picked up scores of passengers, a small restaurant, a tiny park with a public boat-launching area, and an ice-skating rink in winter, are all that remain to remind the visitor of the once vast amusement center.

As the city grew, so did the number of recreational activities available. Tennis appealed to both men and women, and courts were constructed at many of the city parks.

Golf became a popular sport in the early 1900's. At one time it was considered a rich man's game; the earliest golf courses were those at private clubs. The first of these in Grand Rapids appears to have been Kent Country Club which by 1901 was located at the College Avenue site it has occupied ever since. Within a few years the city began to develop municipal golf courses at which the public could play for a small fee. The largest of these was Indian Trails Golf Course on Kalamazoo Avenue which has attracted many golfers each year since its opening in the late 1920's.

Kent Country Club in the early 1900's.

Around the turn of the century, bicycle riding was one of the most popular diversions in Grand Rapids as well as the rest of the nation. The invention of the low-wheel safety bicycle made it possible for people of all ages to enjoy cycling; the original models with the tall front wheel could be maneuvered only by skilled and daring riders.

Some of these early riders formed clubs. The members of one such organization, the Wolverine Bicycle Club, posed for the photograph below while resting on the grass at John Ball Park.

The Wolverine Bicycle Club, 1895.

Hayride along the Thornapple River, 1895.

Another popular activity, in the days before the automobile, was touring the countryside in a horse-drawn wagon or sleigh. The prim and proper women seated in the rear of the wagon are reminders of the stricter morality of those days, when young men and women participating in such activities were carefully chaperoned.

In the last decade of the 1800's, local groups or visitors to Grand Rapids could hire the Furniture City Barge for excursions through the city.

The heavy snows and ice of wintertime were a source of pleasure to many people. Children, as well as many adults, have always enjoyed sledding and tobogganing, ice skating, or just a friendly snowball fight. In those earlier days, however, it was possible to close off hilly streets for sleds and toboggans. Even more remote from modern-day activities were races between horse-drawn sleighs that could be held in main city thoroughfares. Jefferson Avenue and other city streets, as well as the Grand River and occasionally Reeds Lake, were all utilized as winter racetracks. From the number of observers, many on skates, these races were obviously popular events.

Horse-drawn sleigh race on Reeds Lake, 1890's.

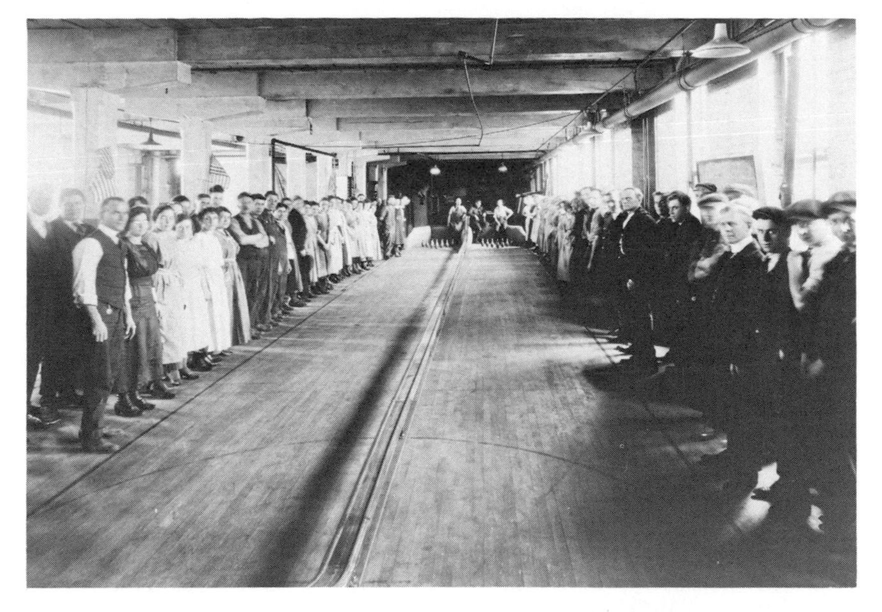

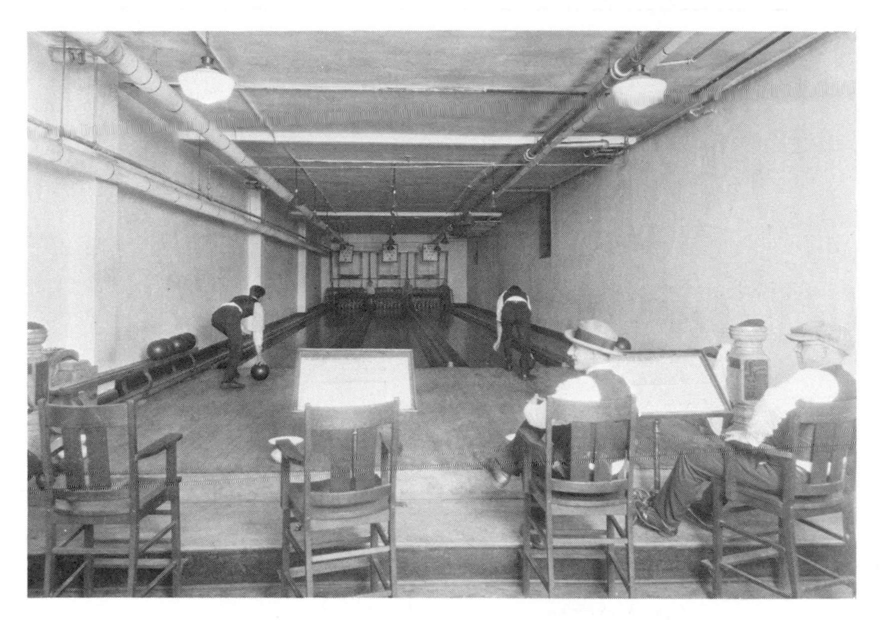

For those with an aversion to the cold of winter, there were activities to enjoy indoors. Bowling was one of these, although it appears to have been frowned upon by the earliest settlers; an ordinance passed in 1838 prohibited the construction of bowling alleys within the village limits. By the 1850's the city fathers had relented and passed regulations concerning the operation of bowling alleys. As the years went by, bowling became an increasingly popular activity enjoyed by the whole family.

Billiard parlors were regulated by ordinance in the same year as bowling establishments but took many more years to gain the same respectability. Billiards were played and enjoyed by many well-to-do families who could buy a table for their homes, but billiard parlors, or pool halls, were disdained by "nice" people for decades, and were not open to women or children. Only in more recent years have "family-type" billiard parlors been established.

Before television brought professional and collegiate athletics into our living rooms, people were more likely to venture out on a weekend afternoon or evening to see a variety of local teams. Grand Rapids has been home to a number of professional teams in sports such as baseball, basketball, and hockey. Sports fans, however, have usually reserved their fiercest loyalties for their high school and college teams. Many Grand Rapidians possess pictures like these in their dens or attics, and treasure the memory of participation in amateur athletics. Few of us will ever forget, whatever our age, the enthusiasm and excitement the contests generated.

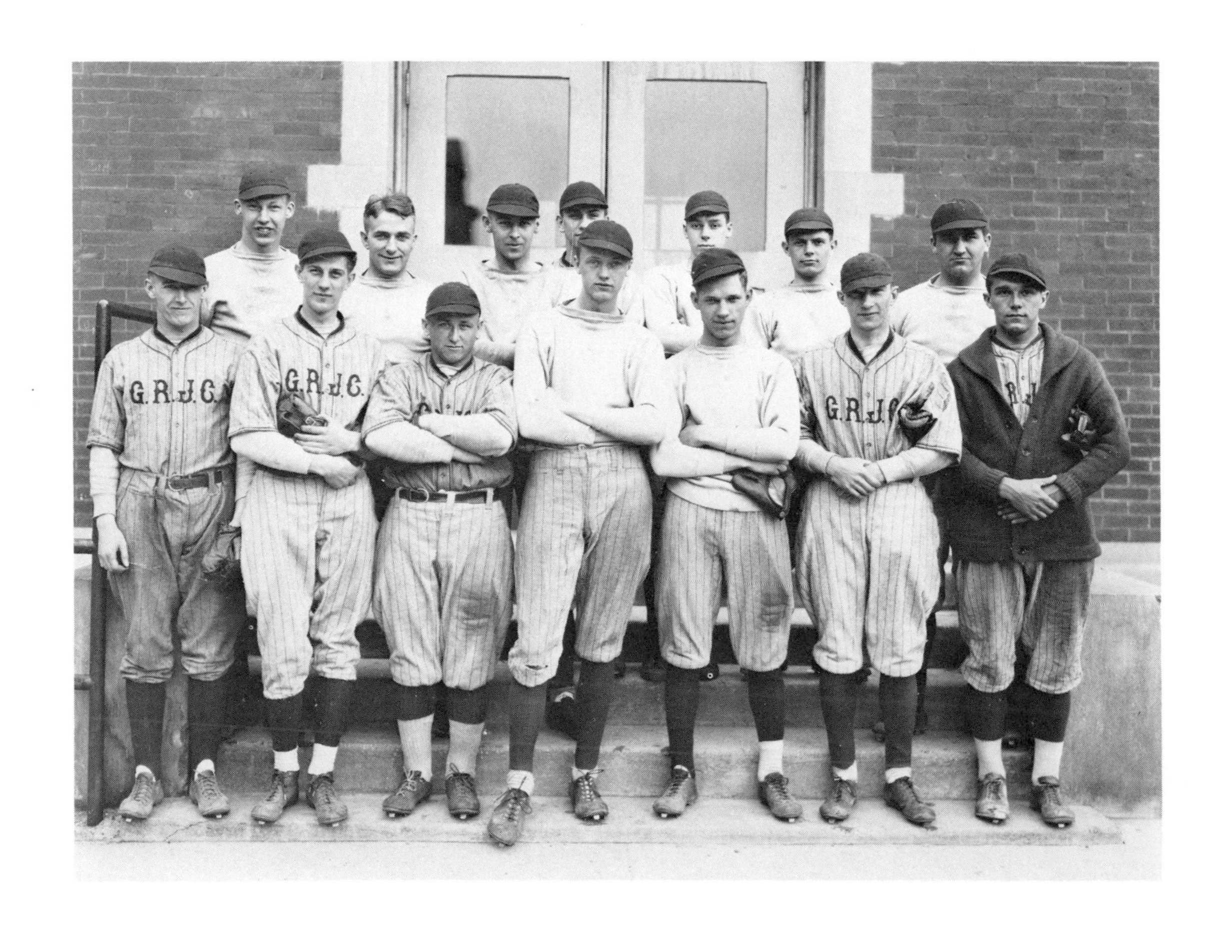

Marching up Canal Street (now Lower Monroe), 1881

Elks' parade.

For many decades perhaps the greatest "spectator sport" of all was the parade. The marching bands with their beating drums and blaring trumpets along with the gaily decorated floats provided a spectacle enjoyed by the thousands that lined the streets. No occasion was missed to organize a parade, including holidays, annual reviews of the police and fire departments, and fund-raising drives, not to mention numerous parades held by conventioneers visiting the city. Like the parades, a circus in town always drew large, excited crowds.

Circus grounds, John Ball Park, 1905.

The Old Yellow Warehouse.

Theater became an integral part of the entertainment scene early in the history of the city. Although the history of the Old Yellow Warehouse, built in 1834, is somewhat vague, it was probably the first building used as a theater. Some of the hotels in the mid-1800's also provided rooms in which theatrical productions could be staged.

The real beginning of professional theater could probably be dated from 1874 with the opening of the lavishly decorated Powers' Grand Opera House, located on Pearl Street near Monroe. It burned, was rebuilt, and was renovated a number of times until it came down to us as the Midtown Theater which finally closed in 1975. The theater in its heyday presented not only the opera of road companies but also serious plays. Performers such as Lillian Russell and Ethel Barrymore appeared on its stage until the 1930's when it began to show films.

1889. Merry Christmas TO ALL.

POWERS' GRAND OPERA HOUSE

FRED BERGER, . . . Lessee and Manager.
FRANK H. COBB, . . . Acting Manager.

SECOND ANNUAL TOUR
722 TO 725 TIMES.

Two Nights With Grand Christmas Day Matinee!

Beginning Tuesday, Dec. 24.

DANIEL FROHMAN'S
NEW YORK
Lyceum Theatre Wife Company,

Presenting the Famous Original four Act Society Comedy by David Belasco and Henry C. DeMille, Authors of "Lord Chumley," "The Charity Ball," Etc.

THE WIFE

CAST OF CHARACTERS.

JOHN RUTHERFORD, of the United State Senate..........Mr. BOYD PUTNAM
MATHEW CULVER, in politics..........Mr. HENRY HERMAN
ROBERT GRAY, attorney at law..........Mr. S. MILLER KENT
SILAS TRUMAN, of the Produce Exchange..........Mr. HENRY TALBOT
MAJOR HOMER Q. PUTNAM, G. A. R., whose "faint heart ne'er won ....Mr. THOMAS H. BURNS
fair lady"..........Mr. STANLEY RIGNOLD
JACK DEXTER, Columbia, '88..........Mr. A. W. GREGORY
MR. RANDOLPH, Rutherford's private secretary..........Miss FRANCES GAUNT
LUCILLE FERRANT, from New Orleans..........Miss ETHEL GREYBROOKE
MRS. S. BELLAMY IVES, in charities..........Miss ETTA HAWKINS
KITTY IVES, coming out..........Miss ELIZA LOGAN
MRS. AMORY, junior member of Truman & Co..........Miss OLIVE DUNTON
AGNES, Helen's maid..........
—AND—
HELEN TRUMAN, an only daughter..........Mrs. BERLAN-GIBBS

SYNOPSIS OF SCENES,

ACT. I—Mrs. Ives' Villa, Newport. July. The amature theatrical. The old affair. "The Lover."

ACT II—Reception Room at Senator Dexter's, Washington. February. Mrs. Dexter's Ball. The Quarrel. "The husband."

ACT III—Library in Rutherford's House, Washington. Same Evening. The investigation. The confession. "The marriage tie." Midnight view of the Capitol.

(The curtain will remain down for two minutes only.)

ACT IV—Same scene. April. The eclipse. The mission to St. Petersburg. "The Wife-"

Scenery from original models of Mr. W. H. Day, art director of the Lyceum Theatre.
Incidental music composed by Mr. Henry Puerner.

FRANK WILLIAMS.......... } For DANIEL FROHMAN { ....AGENT
GEORGE C. BOWERS.......... } For DANIEL FROHMAN { ...BUSINESS MANAGER
A. W. GREGORY.......... } For DANIEL FROHMAN { ....STAGE MANAGER

Mr. Daniel Frohman's other attractions this year are Mr. and Mrs. Kendal, "Our Flat," "Sweet Lavender," Mark Twains' "Prince and Pauper," his Stock Company, now playing "The Charity Ball," at the home Theatre, and Mr. E. H. Sothern.

Powers' Grand Opera House playbill, 1889.

The Empress Theater, 1914.

For those more interested in vaudeville, the Empress Theater at Lyon and Bond was built in 1914. Troops of vaudevillian stars amused Grand Rapids audiences until "talking pictures" replaced vaudeville and diminished the popularity of live theater.

As were many downtown theaters, the Isis on Lower Monroe was first a vaudeville playhouse and then a movie theater; but in the 1930's the Isis was remodeled for legitimate theater. The Grand Rapids Civic Players used this playhouse until it was torn down in the urban renewal project of the 1960's. The Civic Theater then moved to its present location on Leonard Street.

The excitement and fascination generated by the new medium, the "talking picture", is reflected in the advertisements covering the front of this theater.

Another of the elegant downtown theaters was the Regent at Crescent and Bond. It was built in 1923 primarily for movies at a cost thought to be close to one million dollars. The theater included a rooftop garden for ballroom dancing.

The small neighborhood theaters were also popular. They were particularly well-liked by young children who could walk from their homes to the Saturday matinee to see a series of cartoons and an adventure film while they munched on popcorn and candy.

George Welsh, then the City Manager, had the Civic Auditorium built during the Great Depression as a relief work project. The auditorium has been the site of many exciting entertainments including circuses, ice follies, auto shows, boxing matches, and performances of the Grand Rapids Symphony Orchestra. The facilities of the Civic have helped Grand Rapids maintain its reputation as a leading convention city. In 1975 the auditorium was renamed George W. Welsh Civic Auditorium.

In the 1920's radio became an essential element of communication—for the first time news could be received as it happened. Radio also added a large measure of entertainment that could be enjoyed at home, bringing sports events, comedy, and drama into the living room.

Many entertainers became popular through their radio programs and some of them made personal appearances in Grand Rapids. Amos and Andy posed for publicity shots in front of a large crowd of people waiting to see them perform at the Keith Theater.

The list of leisure-time "things-to-do" in Grand Rapids is endless. The young and thriving city offered something for everyone.

Crocheting club, Franklin School Social Center (top); enjoying 3-D views through stereoscopes (middle left); ice-skating on Reeds Lake (middle right); County Commissioner, Harry White, transporting his Sunday School group to a picnic in his chain-driven Mack auto, 1909 (bottom).

Farmer's Market

Life Styles and Neighborhoods

Shantytown, the West Side, the Hill District, the Sixth Ward, South Division–these names revive images of different city neighborhoods, often defined by ethnic boundaries. Over the decades changing patterns of work, shopping, transportation, entertainment, social mobility, immigration, and urban decline and renewal have altered some neighborhoods drastically while others have retained much of their past intact.

Grand Rapids was a young bustling town by the 1870's, but its rural character persisted on the outskirts. This view from the West Bridge Street hill shows the faint outline of the city in the background.

Shantytown, in the middle of this photograph, was the name given to the tough neighborhood south of Monroe near the river where the French and Irish lumberjacks lived. Charles Belknap in his *Yesterdays of Grand Rapids* noted that "the steamer passenger's first glimpse of Shantytown left him in doubt as to whether he was landing in Killarney or Montreal."

Wooden sidewalks and gravel roads were the byways and highways of Grand Rapids in the 1870's.

A restaurant-saloon is visible above in this view down the street from the old Grand Rapids and Indiana Union Depot at the corner of Island and Ionia avenues.

Plainfield Avenue was in the process of being rebuilt when the photograph at right was taken. The old Detroit and Milwaukee depot is barely visible in the upper right corner of the photo.

Lyon Street is in the foreground of this 1870's panorama of the city (above). Note the mixture of large mansions with more modest middle-income dwellings.

In July, 1873, a devastating fire destroyed a large section on the northeast side of the city. The photographs at left and on the next page show the area before, during, and after the fire. The burned out neighborhood, in which more than 125 families had lost their homes, was quickly rebuilt.

Changing neighborhoods can be seen in these photographs of Leonard Street in the 1870's, overlooking the old Detroit and Milwaukee Railroad Station, and Plainfield Avenue in the 1920's.

West Leonard Street market, looking north.

Looking south on Plainfield Avenue, 1920's.

Plainfield and Coit avenues were outside the city limits in the 1880's. By 1950 this intersection had become the hub of a neighborhood shopping district.

Bostwick Avenue was a prosperous neighborhood in the 1880's. The famous Bostwick Elms are visible in all three views. In the 1920's Bostwick Avenue remained a residential area but downtown expansion was edging in by the 1950's.

Grand Rapids of the early 1900's was a city of small clustered neighborhoods that made it the choice of *Survey* magazine in 1920 as a typical small American city.

Looking north from Belknap Park.

Hall Street hill overlooking Pleasant Valley.

Looking west from Hall Street hill.

In the midst of these changing neighborhoods, a variety of institutions, happenings, and customs developed. Some of these are illustrated below and on the following five pages.

City Market, Island Park, 1916.

Martin Hayes' Bar on S. Division in the 1910's.

The Our Theater was a typical neighborhood entertainment center that was located in a commercial district.

Leonard Street near Alpine.

Above is the Grand Rapids' Italian Band on one of its many neighborhood stops.

The nineteenth century produced its share of newsboys prepared to hawk an "extra" in local neighborhoods.

Cold lemonade, neighborhood style, was a common sight during the summer months.

Families played and worked together. Three generations of Ryskamp's (above) shared the work load of a paint and wallpaper business which continued until 1975 on Eastern Avenue.

City meets country in an unexpected fashion in the 1920's photograph below.

As early as the 1910's the gas station moved onto corner lots on main thoroughfares in the city.

Spring cleaning was expedited in elaborate fashion with new techniques that proved to be a neighborhood attraction.

Oakhill Cemetery, pictured below, on Hall Street between Union and Eastern, was one of the city's earliest cemeteries.

House moving produced its own special difficulties for these determined though seemingly somewhat overshadowed workers.

Community cooperation is evident in this photograph of an unidentified but probably typical street junction after a snowstorm.

A Consumers Ice Truck delivers a load of its perishable products.

The brick house on the right above was the residence of Dr. Alonzo Platt, a Grand Rapids physician in the mid-nineteenth century. His 1850 house of stone construction was one of many fine homes built in this fashion.

The two-story stone house below was built in 1846 by Eliphalet B. Turner, one of the first village clerks. One of the first permanent residences on the west side, the Turner house was large and expensive and represented an upper-middle-class style of life.

A local beer maker, Christopher Kusterer, poses in front of his house located near his brewery. The white picket fence and the imposing front porch, with its supporting columns, give evidence of the prosperity of the owner.

By the 1870's and 1880's a much more ornate and decorative style graced upper-class homes. This house at 71 Lafayette, with its male occupants posing in front and a Black servant standing at the side, was typical of many larger homes that were built close to the center of the city.

During the 1880's middle-class housing was clustered along unpaved roads such as Terrace Avenue on the east side. Despite narrow frontages of twenty-five to forty feet, three stories provided abundant living space.

A newly built group of middle-class homes on the west side of Grand Rapids shows the more standardized production methods in vogue by 1910. (Note the house being constructed in the background.) This style of construction allowed a splitting of the house into two vertical sections to house two families, although these particular homes are probably single-family units.

These three middle-class homes, built in southeast Grand Rapids at different times between 1910 and 1950, are part of the urban expansion of the twentieth century. A new type of house, smaller and more functional, with larger lots and garages, was part of the urban pattern in Grand Rapids.

The scene above is a working-class neighborhood on the east side looking toward the Grand River. Note the close proximity to the riverside factories. The three separate chimneys on the house at the left indicate three separate family dwellings on the same lot.

When black laborers were recruited to work in Comstock's pail and tub factory in the 1860's, segregated and crowded housing was provided in "Comstock Row" west of Canal Street near Leonard.

View in 1873, including Comstock Row near the river.

A working-class neighborhood was photographed when the 1904 flood brought havoc and danger to the west side residents. Some residents can be viewed fleeing their flooded homes in the vicinity of Eighth and Turner streets.

Other westsiders lived in less desirable housing on the main commercial thoroughfares as pictured during the 1904 flood at Pearl and Front streets. The proprietors of the stores often lived above their own shops.

Some were more affluent.

Diverse life styles, income and social status are reflected in the residences of Grand Rapids.

1962.

1964.

Originally made up of residences that spanned out from Grab Corners, the fringes of downtown gradually expanded as the commerce and industry of the city grew. Although downtown and commercial, rather than residential in character, the urban renewal of the 1960's represented the single most impressive change in the neighborhoods of Grand Rapids.

The meeting of two centuries, the 19th and the 20th, is represented in this midday photo of the clocks on the old City Hall Building and the Old Kent Bank Tower. Unfortunately, by 1975 only the contemporary clock was still standing.

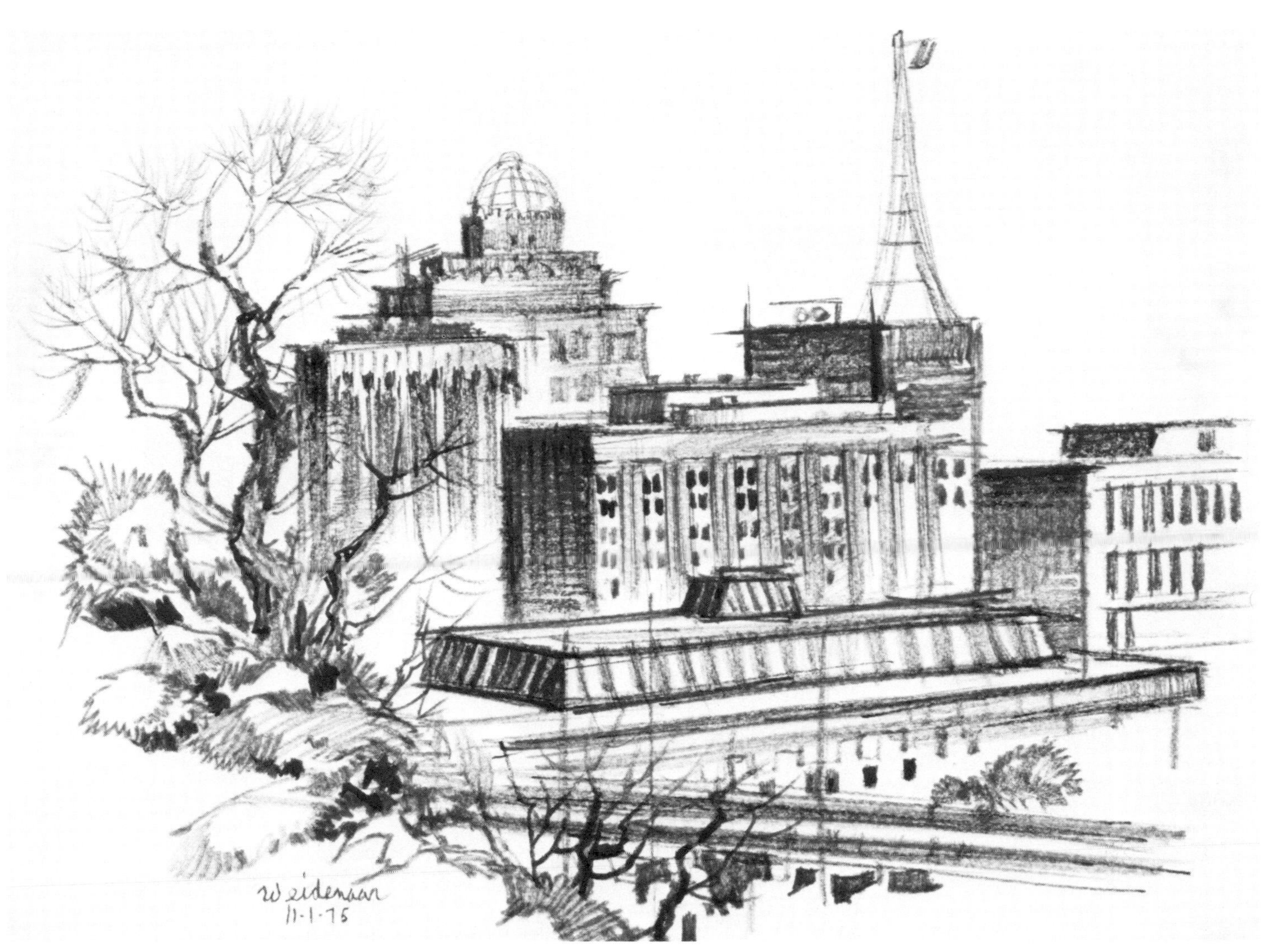

Skyline - Southward from Belknap

Grand Rapids Today

The decision of Louis Campau in 1826 to open a trading post on the shore near the rapids in the Grand River gave birth to the city. By 1975 Grand Rapids had matured into a dynamic economic, political, and social center for western Michigan. The choices made today concerning such things as the future of the downtown area, the quality of life in the neighborhoods, the locations of factories and businesses, and the extent of government services will determine Grand Rapids' course in the near and distant future.

The physical structure of the city is a constantly changing mosaic which has a profound influence on our work and on our leisure-time activities. The decisions of government officials, businessmen, and social leaders are the driving force which sustains the continual modification of the urban structures. The result is a pattern of continuity and change that compels a city to keep recreating itself in a new image to meet the needs of each succeeding generation of citizens. The central business district, for example, is a mixture of decline and hopeful signs of a new revitalization.

Despite the fact that downtown Grand Rapids is no longer a center for hotels, due to the automobile and decentralization, the Pantlind Hotel carries on in its proud tradition. Increasingly dependent on the convention trade, this single remaining full-service hotel continues to be successful. In the photograph above, conventioneers of the Order of the Eastern Star gather in the lobby of the Pantlind. For those who wish to return to the past during a lunch hour or for an evening, the Pantlind offers the Back Room Saloon (below left). Its decor reminds one of an 1890's drinking establishment. The Pantlind also hosts many banquets each year in its Grand Ballroom and other halls. In the photograph at right below, Richard VanderVeen, Congressman from Michigan's 5th District, attends a political fund-raising dinner.

Looking up Monroe Avenue from Campau Square.

Lunch counter at Kresge's.

Jewelry department at Steketee's.

Several empty stores just up the block from the Pantlind Hotel testify to the fact that Monroe Avenue has declined somewhat in importance as a retail market. Yet thousands of people still make purchases there each day. There are plans afoot to make the downtown shopping area more competitive with the suburban malls.

The range of goods and services still available on Monroe Avenue is typified by the short-order counter at Kresge's and the jewelry counter at Steketee's Department Store. Both these retail establishments have long traditions of service in the downtown area.

McKay Tower on Campau Square.

Looking down Monroe Avenue from Monument Park.

Despite the construction of new buildings on North Ottawa, Monroe Avenue continues to be a prime location for professional and business offices. The management and tenants of the McKay Tower, located on historic Campau Square, continue to carry on the qualities of service that were first begun in the 1920's

Looking down Monroe Avenue from Monument Park with its reminder of the sacrifices made by Grand Rapids' citizens during the Civil War, we realize how little the street has changed over the years. Herpolsheimer's occupies a fairly new building and the streetcars have been replaced by buses, but most of the buildings date from the late Victorian period.

Just off Monroe Avenue, on the corner of Ottawa and Pearl, is the old Victorian Ledyard Building. Built in 1874, it is perhaps one of the best reminders of the continuity in Grand Rapids' downtown area.

Across the street on Ottawa is the historic and exclusive Peninsular Club founded in 1881. Over the years the decisions made by its members while eating lunch have shaped the destiny of the city.

The Ledyard Building.

The Peninsular Club.

Down a few blocks from the "Penn" Club on Ottawa Avenue is the urban redevelopment area which broke with the past in the late 1960's in order to create a new, contemporary look. It provides utilitarian office space for business and government. Vandenberg Plaza contains two of the city's art treasures, both by the world-renowned artist, Alexander Calder. *La Grande Vitesse* is an imposing red metal stabile in front of City Hall; on the roof of the County Building is an abstract painting.

Once a year the plaza is the site of a truly city-wide celebration. Thousands gather to eat ethnic food, listen and watch local performers, and participate in a myriad of activities. For a short time a metamorphosis takes place in which the impersonal city is transformed into its historic communal village form. There is a spirit of happiness and friendship in the air.

Festival '74, Vandenberg Plaza.

I-196, the Gerald R. Ford Freeway.

With the speed and convenience of the city's expressways, many people now live in the communities around Grand Rapids and shop at one of the many new malls.

Of the more than a dozen shopping centers developed in the area, beginning with Rogers Plaza in September, 1961, Woodland Mall is one of the largest.

Rogers Plaza.

Woodland Mall.

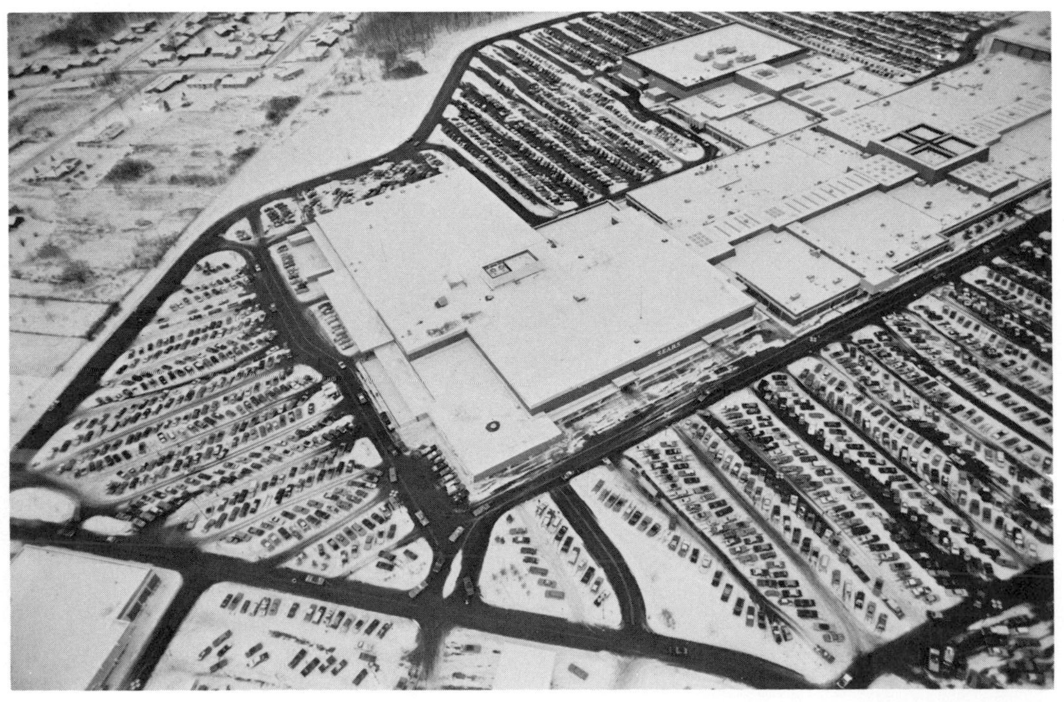

The malls, in addition to containing many fine stores, hold shows and exhibits. In the photograph above, Woodland Mall is the site of a demonstration of classic automobiles. Woodland Mall also houses an important piece of art, *Split Ring* by Clement Meadmore, the sculpture in the photograph below. Thus the various shopping malls provide some of the services of the old village squares. Contemporary advantages of the malls include acres of free parking and total climate-controlled shopping.

Between Rogers Plaza and Eastbrook Mall stretches 28th Street. As one drives along the busy street, it seems that the principal business is fast-order food franchises. Prominent among the eighty or so restaurants is the popular McDonald's hamburger chain. The proliferation of such restaurants is a result of shifting eating patterns among Americans. Young people who have cars and wish to eat away from their families, and young married couples and their children who wish to eat out cheaply and informally, are the chief patrons.

Fulton Street Farmer's Market.

At the same time that fast-order restaurants flourish, those who prefer their produce fresh from the farm continue to shop at the Fulton Street Farmer's Market. Here one can capture some of the spirit of old-time village life as the farmer and the buyer meet face-to-face to talk over the merits and price of available fruits and vegetables. Most people, however, shop at the many modern supermarkets in Grand Rapids.

Grand Rapids parks continue to offer pleasant surroundings for recreation and relaxation. In the case of Veterans' Memorial Park, we are also reminded to honor the city's war dead who sacrificed so much. The parks, due to the changing patterns of leisure-time activities, are not used as much per capita as they once were. Yet we owe a debt of gratitude to our forebears who had the vision to set aside some green spaces in the growing concrete and asphalt of the city for continued use by the generations to follow.

Veterans' Memorial Park.

Duck pond at John Ball Park.

Aquinas College.

As urban life has become more complex, the need for highly trained professionals in public employment and private business has become more apparent. For a city its size, Grand Rapids is almost unique in that it has such a large number of academically recognized institutions of higher learning. Pictured here are Aquinas, a four-year independent liberal arts college, restructured in 1940 from a junior college founded in 1922; Calvin, a four-year Christian Reformed college and seminary founded in 1921; Grand Rapids Junior College, a two-year college founded in 1914; Davenport College of Business, a two-year business college founded in 1924; and Kendall School of Design, founded in 1928. Grand Valley State Colleges, founded in 1962 and located in Allendale, a town just outside Grand Rapids, has become widely known for its cluster college concept of education. Also in Grand Rapids are St. Joseph Seminary, Grand Rapids Baptist College and Seminary, Reformed Bible College, Grace Bible College, Grand Rapids School of the Bible and Music, and several university extension services. With such an array of educational institutions, the future of Grand Rapids in a technological and rapidly changing age is assured.

Calvin College.

Grand Rapids Junior College.

Davenport College of Business.

Kendall School of Design.

Railroad warehouse on Campau near Fulton

Grand Rapids, although no longer served by interurban passenger railroad service, continues to be the transportation hub of western Michigan. Freight trains, fleets of trucks, and many air cargo services offer fast delivery world-wide. The movement of people via bus and plane increases yearly.

Greyhound Bus terminal south of Monroe on Market.

Recent relocation and expansion of Kent County Airport have facilitated the access and egress of large jet aircraft. North Central and United airlines offer Grand Rapids passengers an increasing number of direct flights to major cities as well as connecting flights to anywhere and everywhere.

Fisher Body Plant No. 2.

American Seating Company.

The city has maintained its diversified economic base with automobile parts, furniture, and banking playing leading roles.

A suburban branch of Union Bank.

On a typical fall weekday in Grand Rapids in 1975, while many residents were hard at work, others were enjoying themselves on the Grand River watching or attempting to catch Coho salmon near the new fish ladder and riverside beautification project.

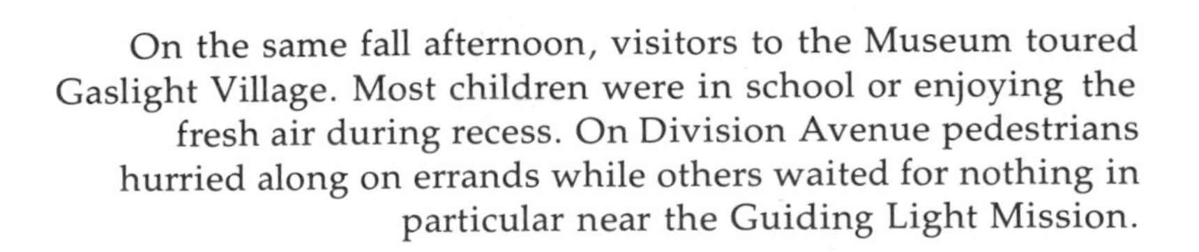

On the same fall afternoon, visitors to the Museum toured Gaslight Village. Most children were in school or enjoying the fresh air during recess. On Division Avenue pedestrians hurried along on errands while others waited for nothing in particular near the Guiding Light Mission.

St. Andrew's Cathedral.

True Light Baptist Church.

Highland Hills Christian Reformed Church.

Fifth Reformed Church.

Grand Rapids maintains its reputation as a city of churches. Some of the city's most interesting architecture is found in its church buildings. Older ornate structures, many in the Gothic style, contrast sharply with newer structures with clean contemporary lines.

St. Andrew's, the first Catholic church in town, became a cathedral with the establishment in 1882 of the Grand Rapids Diocese. The current structure was rebuilt in 1903 after a fire. Built more recently along contemporary lines, the True Light Baptist Church, originally organized in 1922, serves a predominately Black congregation. The descendants of immigrants from Holland still support many churches, especially the Reformed Church in America and Christian Reformed denominations. Pictured here are Highland Hills Christian Reformed Church and Fifth Reformed Church, the latter with a history dating back ninety years.

The many contemporary church structures in Grand Rapids testify to the continued vitality of religious life in the city.

Grand Rapids in March, 1975.

These pictures end in 1975, but the changes of the past that they highlight will continue into the future. The physical structures of the city will be altered in significant ways. The pictures also demonstrate the continuity of the past into the present. In order to maximize the possibilities of a good life in Grand Rapids, what is best in our past should be preserved while daring alterations in the way we do things should also be encouraged. What we do today will become part of Grand Rapids' history tomorrow.

Picture Credits and Acknowledgments

The editors would like to express their appreciation for the invaluable assistance of the individuals and institutions who provided the illustrations used in this book. Every effort has been made to identify the source for each illustration. In the picture credit list below, the following abbreviations have been used: CV - Craig VanderLende, Photographer; L - Grand Rapids Public Library (General Collection); LF - Grand Rapids Public Library (Fitch Collection); LH - Grand Rapids Public Library (Hooper Collection); LJ - Grand Rapids Public Library (Johnston Collection); LM - Grand Rapids Public Library (Morris Collection); M - Grand Rapids Public Museum.

DOWNTOWN:
13 Weidenaar; **14** top - LH; **14** center - LH; **14** bottom - LH; **15** top left - LH; **15** top right - LH; **15** bottom - LH; **16** top - LH; **16** bottom - LH; **17** top - L; **17** bottom left - LH; **17** bottom right - M; **18** top left - LH; **18** top right - LH; **18** bottom - H; **19** top - LJ; **19** center - LJ; **19** bottom - L; **20** top - LJ; **20** center - L; **20** bottom - L; **21** top - M; **21** center left - L; **21** center right - L; **21** bottom - M; **22** - L; **23** top - LH; **23** bottom - M; **24** top - M; **24** center - M; **24** bottom - LM; **25** top - LH; **25** center - LH; **25** bottom - LH; **26** top - LF; **26** bottom - L; **27** top - M; **27** center - L; **27** bottom - M; **28** top - M; **28** center - M; **28** bottom - M; **29** top left - M; **29** top right - M; **29** bottom - M; **30** top - M; **30** bottom left - M; **30** bottom right - M.

GOVERNMENT SERVES THE PEOPLE:
31 - Weidenaar; **32** - M; **33** top - L; **33** bottom - L; **34** top - LH; **34** center - M; **34** bottom - LM; **35** top - LH; **35** bottom - L; **36** top - Rev. Edward Boone; **36** center - M; **36** bottom - M; **37** top - L; **37** center - M; **37** bottom - M; **38** top - L; **38** bottom - LJ; **39** top - L; **39** bottom - L; **40** top left - L; **40** top right - L; **40** center - L; **40** bottom left - L; **40** bottom right -L; **41** top left - M; **41** top right -L; **41** center left - L; **41** center right - L; **41** bottom - L; **42** top - L; **42** center left - L; **42** center right - L; **42** bottom left - L; **42** bottom right -L; **43** top left - L; top right - L; **43** center - L; bottom -L; **44** top left - M; top right - M; bottom -L; **45** top - M; center - LH; bottom - LH; **46** top - L; middle - LH; bottom - M; **47** top - LF; bottom - LJ; **48** top - LJ; bottom - L; **49** top - L; center - L; bottom - L; **50** top - L; center - L; bottom - L; **51** top - L; bottom - L; **52** top - LF; **52** center - LM; bottom - L; **53** top - M; center - M; bottom left - M; bottom right - M; **54** top - M; center - M; bottom - LM; **55** top - M; center - M; bottom - LG; **56** top M; top left - M; center left - M; bottom left - M; **57** top - LH; **57** top center - LH; **57** bottom center - LH; **57** bottom left - LH; **57** bottom right - LH; **58** top - L; **58** middle - LH; **58** bottom - L; **59** top - M; **59** center - LM; **59** bottom left - LM; **59** bottom right - M; **60** top - L; **60** center - M; **60** bottom - LJ; **61** top - LM; **61** center - M; **61** bottom - Grand Rapids Area Chamber of Commerce; **62** top - The White House; **62** bottom - CV.

WORKERS AND INDUSTRY:
63 - Weidenaar; **64** top - LJ; **64** bottom - LH; **65** top - LH; **65** bottom - L; **66** all - LH; **67** top - L; **67** center - LH; **67** bottom - L; **68** top - L; **68** bottom - L; **69** top - M; **69** center - M; **69** bottom - M; **70** top - M; **70** bottom - L; **71** top - M; **71** center - LH; **71** bottom - M; **72** top - LF; **72** center - L; **72** bottom - L; **73** top - M; **73** center - M; **73** bottom - L; **74** top - L; **74** bottom - Rowland Schreiber; **75** top - LH; **75** center - LH; **75** bottom - LH; **76** top - L; **76** bottom - M; **77** top - M; **77** bottom - M; **78** top - M; **78** bottom - M; **79** top - L; **79** bottom - LF; **80** top left - L; **80** top right - L; **80** center - L; **80** bottom - Franklin W. Ryskamp; **81** top - L; **81** center - Kenneth Hicks; **81** bottom - LM; **82** top left - M; **82** top right - M; **82** center - M; **82** bottom - M; **83** top - M; **83** bottom - M; **84** top - L; **84** center - L; **84** bottom - M; **85** top left - L; **85** top right - L; **85** center - L; **85** bottom - M; **86** - M.

GETTING FROM HERE TO THERE:
87 Weidenaar, **88** Everett Swanson, **89** - LH; **90** top - LH; **90** center - LH; **90** bottom - LH; **91** top left - LH; **91** top right - LH; **91** bottom - LH; **92** top - LH; **92** center - LJ; **92** bottom - LH; **93** top left - LH; **93** top right - L; **93** bottom - LJ; **94** top - LH; **94** center - L; **94** bottom - LH; **95** top - LH; **95** center - LH; **95** bottom - LH; **96** top left - LH; **96** top right - LH; **96** bottom - L; **97** top - LH; **97** center - LH; **97** bottom - LH; **98** top - M; **98** center - LH; **98** bottom - M; **99** top - M; **99** bottom - M; **100** top - LF; **100** bottom - LJ; **101** top - M; **101** center - M; **101** bottom - M; **102** top - L; **102** center - L; **102** bottom - L; **103** top - LJ; **103** bottom - M; **104** top left - LM; **104** top right - LM; **104** bottom - M; **105** top left - M; **105** top right - M; **105** bottom - M; **106** top - M; **106** center - M; **106** bottom - M; **107** top - M; **107** center - M; **107** bottom - M; **108** top left - M; **108** top right - LM; **108** center - L; **108** bottom - M; **109** top - M; **109** center - M; **109** bottom left - M; **109** bottom right - M; **110** to p - Lewis N. Steenwyk; **110** center - M; **110** bottom left - L; **110** bottom right - M.

CHURCHES AND ORGANIZATIONS:
111 Weidenaar; **112** top - LJ; **112** center - Baxter, *History of Grand Rapids;* **112** bottom - LH; **113** top - LH; **113** bottom - LJ; **114** top - LM; **114** bottom - LM; **115** top left - LM; **115** top right - LM; **115** bottom - M; **116** top left - LM; **116** top right - LM; **116** center - LM; **116** bottom - M; **117** top - Lewis N. Steenwyk; **117** bottom left - M; **117** bottom right - M; **118** top - M; **118** bottom - M; **119** top - M; **119** bottom - M; **120** top - M; **120** center - M; **120** bottom - M; **121** top - Lewis N. Steenwyk; **121** bottom - M; **122** top - M; **122** center - L; **122** bottom - M; **123** top left - L; **123** top right - LM; **123** bottom - LM; **124** top left - L; **124** top right - LM; **124** bottom - M; **125** top - M; **125** bottom left - St. Cecilia Music Society; **125** bottom right - St. Cecilia Music Society; **126** top - LM; **126** bottom - M; **127** top - LM; **127** bottom - LM; **128** top - L; **128** center - L; **128** bottom - L.

LEISURE AND ENTERTAINMENT:
129 - Weidenaar; **130** top - M; **130** bottom - LH; **131** top - L; **131** bottom - L; **132** top - M; **132** bottom left - M; **132** bottom right - M; **133** top - M; **133** bottom - L; **134** top - M; **134** bottom - L; **135** top - L; **135** bottom - LH; **136** top - LH; **136** center - LH; **136** bottom - LM; **137** top - M; **137** center - M; **137** bottom - M; **138** top - LH; **138** center - LH; **138** bottom - LH; **139** top - LH; **139** bottom - L; **140** top - M; **140** bottom - LH; **141** top - M; **141** center - M; **141** bottom - M; **142** top - M; **142** center - M; **142** bottom - M; **143** top - L; **143** center - L; **143** bottom - L; **144** top left - Baxter, *History of Grand Rapids;* **144** top right - Anthony Travis; **144** bottom - L; **145** top - L; **145** center - M; **145** bottom - M; **146** top - M; **146** bottom - M; **147** top left - M; **147** top right - M; **147** center - M; **147** bottom - M; **148** top - L; **148** center left - M; **148** center right - L; **148** bottom - Lewis N. Steenwyk.

LIFE STYLES AND NEIGHBORHOODS:
149 - Weidenaar; **150** top - LJ; **150** bottom - LJ; **151** top - LJ; **151** center - LJ; **151** bottom - LJ; **152** top - LJ; **152** center - LF; **152** bottom - LF; **153** top - LF; **153** bottom - LJ; **154** top - M; **154** bottom - M; **155** top - L; **155** bottom - L; **156** top - L; **156** center - L; **156** bottom - L; **157** top - L; **157** bottom - L; **158** top - L; **158** bottom - L; **159** top - L; **159** bottom - L; **160** top - L; **160** center - L; **160** bottom - M; **161** top - Franklin W. Ryskamp; **161** bottom - M; **162** top - M; **162** center - M; **162** bottom - M; **163** top - M; **163** center - M; **163** bottom - M; **164** top L; **164** bottom - L; **165** top - M; **165** bottom - L; **166** top - L; **166** bottom - M; **167** top - L; **167** center - L; **167** bottom - L; **168** top - L; **168** bottom - LF; **169** top - LJ; **169** center - L; **169** bottom - M; **170** top - L; **170** bottom - M; **171** - Czetli Photography; **172** Bernie's Photographs.

GRAND RAPIDS TODAY:
173 - Weidenaar; **174** - all CV; **175** - all CV; **176** - all CV; **177** top - Grand Rapids Press; **177** bottom - CV; **178** - all CV; **179** - all CV; **180** - all CV; **181** all CV; **182** top - CV; **182** bottom - Calvin College; **183** - all CV; **184** - all CV; **185** top - CV; **185** bottom - Kent Co. Airport; **186** - all CV; **187** top - CV; **187** center and bottom - Henry Zeman; **188** - all CV; **189** top left - CV; **189** top right - True Light Baptist Church; **189** center - CV; **189** bottom - Fifth Reformed Church; **190** Czetli Photography.

Publisher's Note: This book was set by Fotoheads in Palatino Roman, with display faces in Palatino Italic and Davida. Printed by Malloy Lithographing, Inc., on 80# Michigan Matte. Bound by Dekker Bookbinders in Columbia BSL #3647. Book design by Catherine Cuti. Dust jacket design by Walter Kerr. Printed by Wobbema Press, Inc.